£5

SYNTHETIC DYEING

SYNTHETIC DYEING

*for spinners, weavers,
knitters and embroiderers*

FRANCES AND TONY TOMPSON

A DAVID & CHARLES CRAFT BOOK

Cover design based on a tapestry by Lynda Robertson
Photography by Arthur Creighton
Line drawings by Eadan Art

British Library Cataloguing in Publication Data

Tompson, Frances
    Synthetic dyeing: for spinners, weavers,
    knitters and embroiderers.
    1. Dyes and dyeing—Textile fibers
    I. Title   II. Tompson, Tony
    746.6   TP904

    ISBN 0-7153-8874-6

Text and illustrations © Frances and Tony Tompson 1987

Typeset by Typesetters (Birmingham) Ltd,
Smethwick, West Midlands
and printed in Great Britain
by Butler & Tanner Limited, Frome and London
for David & Charles Publishers plc
Brunel House   Newton Abbot   Devon

PREFACE

This book is for amateur and professional craftworkers alike – spinners, weavers, embroiderers and knitters – and textile students. It presents simple and tested methods of using synthetic dyes to colour wool, mohair, silk, cotton, rayon, acrylic, nylon and other fibres.

Colours can be bright and clear, pale and mysterious, deep, rich, subtle or muted, just as one wishes. The dyes have good fastness to light and washing, and with care in use can give repeatable colours. Anyone who has used natural dyes and experienced the elation of obtaining unexpected and beautiful tints and shades, only to be saddened when they faded or proved impossible to repeat, will appreciate how great a benefit that is.

Synthetic dyes are made in a variety of types, each designed for a particular group of fibres or method of use. This book is written in simple, non-technical language as far as possible, and covers acid, reactive, metal-complex, direct, disperse and vat dyes, and briefly describes other types such as basic, azoic, chrome and household varieties. It covers yarn and fibre dyeing only, however; cloth dyeing and printing have been omitted because they are already very well covered in other publications.

With this book, spinners will find they can add a touch of colour to a Jacob's fleece, or rainbow-dye a white one, before converting either of them into yarn. Alternatively, they can dye their spun yarn in a choice from many thousand hues, tints and shades.

Weavers can add exciting ikat or dip-dyed effects to the yarn they are using, paint their warp and weft threads, or just produce the exact colours they need for a particular project – even change the colour of yarns already in stock.

Embroiderers can create their own individual and unique effects, while knitters can alter the colour of bought wool, or produce spectacular effects on mixed fibre yarns such as wool/acrylic or acrylic/nylon blends.

Students may find the simple presentation of information and the results of practical experiments a useful addition to the scientific language of textbooks.

Working with synthetic dyes is an exciting and absorbing experience that can be enjoyed by complete novices as well as by more experienced craftspeople who have used similar materials before. The skilful use of dyes can add a new and satisfying dimension to craftwork, and the glow of colour to your textiles.

CONTENTS

For our parents,
Pat and Tassie Watson, and
Walter and Essie Tompson,
who always showed such interest in
our various activities.

1
INTRODUCTION

Synthetic dyeing occupies a comparatively recent place in the history of applying colour to fibres and fabrics. For seven thousand years at least colours were obtained from animal, vegetable or mineral sources, known collectively as the 'natural' dyes. Extracts and solutions were made from these materials and dyeworkers became highly skilled in producing colours to order from a limited range of basic dyes, and in developing reliable methods of applying them. The Minoans in Crete were producing purple dye from sea snails before the Greek civilisation ever existed; Egyptians of the Middle Kingdom were applying madder and weld dyes by methods that have preserved their colours even to the present time; indigo was used in Japan from the seventh century and the natives in Mexico employed cochineal well before the Spanish conquests.

As knowledge spread to Europe, craftsmen dyers emerged in the West. Progressively, they added to the old techniques, acquired fresh skills, and organised themselves into guilds to set and monitor standards and to qualify themselves according to ability. Many of their discoveries have relevance today – the use of chrome, for example, and the application of indigo and vat dyes.

Until the middle of the eighteenth century all this knowledge and ability was directed towards colouring relatively small amounts of cloth at a time, produced by cottage weavers in their own homes. Natural dyes were well suited to this scale of activity and the seasonal changes that can occur in their strength and purity were not important. Variations in colour between one length of cloth and another were quite acceptable until the advent of the Industrial Revolution.

The progressive mechanisation of spinning and weaving processes began to undermine the cottage industry; cloth could be produced more cheaply and in greater quantities than before. Demand grew as more people could afford it, and they in turn became more critical about colour. 'Shade matching' was important and requirements emerged for new 'fashion' colours. Dyers faced with these demands introduced fresh processes in an attempt to keep pace with developments. As time passed, however, they became increasingly hard-pressed by the limitations of the natural dyestuffs, and by the end of the century the situation had become ripe for a change. This change began in a curious way.

A budding chemical industry had also emerged at this time and scientists were seeking practical applications for its new technology. At the Royal College of Chemistry in London, research was being conducted into products based on coal-tar. The work was guided by a Professor Hoffman, who suggested to an 18-year-old student named Perkin that he might explore the possibilities of developing synthetic quinine. Perkin tried several reactions, including one that produced a dark precipitate instead of the drug he was looking for; for some unknown reason he examined this substance more carefully instead of throwing it away, and he discovered that it had a purple colour and would dye silk without the colour washing off.

Purple had always been a colour of importance. It was a symbol of status and power in ancient Rome, and later in Byzantium; it was a mark of authority in the vestments of the early Roman Catholic church, and even today it appears in ceremonial robes worn on State occasions. As a natural dyestuff it was a difficult and expensive colour to make, and Perkin was thus well able to appreciate the importance of his discovery. Against the advice of his professor he set about commercialising his process.

By today's standards Perkin's dye was not particularly fast, but it was a considerable success in France – where it was named *mauveine* after the purple flower of the French mallow – and in Britain where it was called 'mauve'. Queen Victoria had a gown dyed with it which she is said to have worn to the Great Exhibition in 1862, and it was used for many years to produce the light purple colour of the penny postage stamps of the time.

The discovery that a dye could be made in a laboratory instead of being extracted from a natural source aroused a great deal of interest and stimulated research in Britain and in Europe, but it had little immediate effect on the use of natural dyestuffs, which continued as before. However, chemists now began to study dyeplants and to consider what it was in them that produced colour. Their first interest was the madder plant; this gave a dye of considerable importance which had been used from the third century at least as the main source of reds and browns for cotton and wool. In 1826 two chemists identified its colour constituent as alizarin, and shortly after this Perkin in Britain, and Gräbe and Lieberman in Germany found ways, at almost the same time, of making alizarin in the laboratory. This was a far more important discovery than Perkin's mauve as it pointed the way to synthetic dyes that had consistent quality and strength. Other colours soon followed: a magenta called fuchsine was introduced in 1859 in France; a range of reddish-purples appeared in Germany; blues and violets, greens and red all followed between the years 1860 and 1885.

These new colours were based on aniline, a coal-tar derivative. They allowed dye strength and purity to be controlled as never before, making it easier to match colours accurately, and their greater power made them cheaper to use. The development of these substances, deriving from the initial study of madder, marked the real turning point from natural to synthetic dyestuffs.

Aniline or 'basic' dyes unite very readily with animal fibres and especially with silk. They produce brilliant colours, but unfortunately they are not very fast. As other alternative compounds were developed the aniline dyes lost popularity until today they are hardly ever used in textile dyeing in their original form, although they are used to colour leather and grasses, raffia, bark, etc. A modified type was subsequently introduced especially for colouring acrylic and some other man-made fibres.

Because the aniline dyes lacked fastness, chemists looked further for a wool and silk dye that would not fade or wash out, and they approached this quest with the technique of 'mordanting' in mind. A mordant is a metallic salt added during the dyeing sequence to promote an affinity between the dye and the fibre, thus improving fastness. The process had been used for several centuries in natural dyeing – by the ancient Egyptians, for example – and this would have been known by the new dye chemists. By adding a chromium salt to the dyebath they succeeded in producing a synthetic dye with a much improved fastness over the aniline dyes, although colours were somewhat muted. Dyes of this new type were known as 'mordant' or 'chrome' dyes, and were first introduced in 1868; two methods of application were evolved. In the first – the 'afterchrome' process – the mordant is added after completion of the dyeing phase; this obviously is a two-stage process and thus extends the dyeing time. Further research improved on this with the 'metachrome' system in which the mordant and dye are used together in the dyebath. Chrome dyes are still used where high fastness is required, typically for tailoring fabrics where sombre colours are acceptable.

Acid dyes appeared in 1875, and were developed directly from the study and isolation of the dye element in natural dyestuffs, and its production in synthetic form. They were a more effective way of colouring wool, silk and hair, and could be used without a mordant; thus they reduced the costs of dyeing. They need acidic conditions in the dyebath – hence their name – but produce bright colours of good fastness. They are fully covered in Chapter 5.

At the same time that these developments were taking place, similar improvements were being sought in cotton dyeing. Up to this time all cotton dyes needed the assistance of a mordant, thus complicating and extending the dyeing sequence and making it expensive. Ciba-Geigy eventually produced a new compound that could be applied simply and directly to cotton and other cellulose fibres in one operation, and they introduced it in 1883. Colours were bright and clear and the new dyes became known as the 'direct' dyes from the manner of their application. Unfortunately, their fastness to washing is not always of a high order, but they are used for clothing, the cheaper types of cotton goods, sewing cottons and furnishing fabrics. They are the simplest of all dyes to use and are fully dealt with in Chapter 6.

In 1901 vat dyes were developed in Germany. Like indigo and woad, they have to be 'reduced' to an alternative chemical form before they will dissolve in a dyebath and transfer to a fibre. In the days of indigo this was accomplished by fermenting the dye in old wine vats – hence the name – but the process was unsuited to large-scale dyeing. It had long been known that a similar reaction could be induced using the chemical reagent sodium dithionite (sometimes called hydrosulphite or 'hydros' for short), but it was too expensive for commercial use. In 1869 a researcher named Schutzen-berger discovered a cheap way of making hydros, and later in 1880 Bayer succeeded in making synthetic indigo. The knowledge gained from these two developments enabled a whole new family of vat dyes to be introduced, and they are used today in a wide range of types and are notable for their unsurpassed fastness on cotton and other vegetable fibres. Vat dyes are dealt with in Chapter 8.

Azo, or azoic, dyes were discovered in 1880 by a British chemist, Robert Holliday, who was researching the effects of impregnating cotton fibre with one chemical and then treating it with another. His process underwent further refinement and these dyes were introduced in their modern form in 1912. The system is somewhat complicated; the fibre is first treated with a 'coupling' component – a naphthol preparation – and then exposed to a 'diazo' compound, (from which the dyes take their name). Alone, neither of the two components will produce colour, but when brought together on the fibre a chemical reaction, called coupling, takes place and colour results. The colours are bright and very fast, and azo dyes are used for textile printing on dress fabrics, furnishings, canvas, etc.

While vat and, later, azo dyes were being developed for cotton, studies were continuing into better ways of colouring wool, and especially into improvements to the chrome dyes. Eventually, it became possible to unite a chrome atom with the dye compound so that both could be applied at the same time instead of separately; the process was thus simpler and shorter. Because of their chemical structure these dyes are known as the 'pre-metallised' or 'metal-complex' dyes and they were introduced in 1915. They have excellent all-round fastness but, like the chrome dyes from which they were developed, they produce muted colours, very similar to those obtained from natural dyestuffs. This makes them attractive to many craftworkers who prefer the soft hues of natural dyes but appreciate the fastness and repeatability of the synthetic types. Metal-complex dyes are covered in detail in Chapter 5.

Disperse dyes were introduced in 1923 as a means of colouring acetate rayon, which could not be dyed by any existing method. Dyes existed that would colour the fibre but they could not be dissolved in any substance that was compatible with that form of rayon. Chemists evolved a new concept of applying the dyes as suspensions of extremely fine particles in a dyebath, instead of being dissolved. Unhappily, acetate rayon did not become as popular as was expected and the future for disperse dyes was uncertain until the advent of man-made fibres. They were then found to be the only way of colouring some of these materials and have now become a very important class of dye. Methods of applying them are discussed in Chapter 9.

The simplicity of the direct dyes made them cheap and attractive to use, but their mediocre fastness was a problem. Vat and azo dyes overcame the fastness difficulties, but were complicated to apply. Chemists had for many years thought of a compound that might be made to combine chemically with cotton and linen fibres, instead of uniting with them physically. Such a dye was bound to have outstanding fastness and should be straightforward to apply. In 1952 Hoechst introduced such a compound and it was known as a 'fibre-reactive' dye because it reacted with the fibre during the dyeing process. This name was later shortened by convention to simply 'reactive'. The Hoechst dye was intended for colouring wool and its discovery paved the way for the subsequent development of similar dyes for use on cotton. ICI introduced cellulose reactive dyes in 1956 and these were rapidly developed into a number of types that are applied both hot and cold to cotton and wool fibres. They have been one of the most successful dyes producing very bright colours of excellent fastness; they are dealt with in greater detail in Chapter 7.

As the range of dyes grew, so did the ways in which they were used. Today, we colour food and drink, paper and leather, motor-cars and medicines; we stain samples of body tissue to make it easier to detect diseases, and we spray furs to make them seem more attractive. We colour cosmetics and ceramics, printing inks and plastics. Some dye compounds have even been found to have medicinal qualities and are used to combat disease. It has been estimated that in all some 3,000,000 dyes were discovered, of which around 9,000 or so went into production. In 1974 there were 7,000 colours for textiles alone, manufactured under 30,000 different brand names. The industry is vast, yet it all grew in just over 130 years from a chance discovery made in a laboratory in an obscure suburb of London.

Health and safety

All chemicals need to be treated with care and common sense. If they are handled casually, or carelessly stored, or used incorrectly, they can cause harm in the same way that ordinary household substances like bleach, disinfectants and insecticides can be highly dangerous if they are not treated properly.

Synthetic dyes are no different. They present a low risk when handled with reasonable precautions, and there need be no apprehension about them, but if they are misused then they may become harmful. The following simple rules are intended to protect craftworkers, and should be followed by everyone working with synthetic dyes.

---

1 Always wear rubber gloves and an overall or apron. Dyes are not poisons but some people may have sensitive skin and develop a mild reaction to them, such as a reddening or even a rash, if in contact for a significant time. Rubber gloves will prevent this, and at the same time ensure that any small cuts, abrasions, etc are effectively covered.

Apart from these considerations, dyes are meant to dye and can stain hands and fingers unless gloves are worn. Such stains can take several days to wear off.

An apron or, better still, a sleeved overall, will prevent clothing from becoming damaged or stained if dye or dye liquor is accidentally splashed or spilled.

2 Avoid creating or inhaling dust from dry dye powders. Any dust that is inhaled, be it from coal, icing sugar, even face powder, can settle in the respiratory system and cause or aggravate bronchial irritation. Dye powders can have similar effects, but dust from the cold-water reactives is the most potentially harmful. Chapter 7 discusses additional safety precautions that should be applied especially to those dyes.

With all dyes, avoid creating a dust in the first place by handling loose dye gently and carefully, without hurried actions. Most dye powders are treated during manufacture to reduce dusting, but it is not possible to eliminate it altogether, so precautions are necessary. The amount of powder being handled will vary according to the amount of material being dyed, but in most craftwork will amount to no more than a few grams at a time. While this may represent a negligible risk, it is still common sense to wear a simple disposable dustmask while mixing the dyes if there is any chance of dust being inhaled.

3 Avoid inhaling vapours from dyepots. A properly chosen working area will have adequate ventilation to carry away any steam and vapours, and in these circumstances there should be no problems. Nevertheless, it is not wise to inhale the atmosphere immediately above a hot mixing beaker or a dyepot; most vapour will be steam but sometimes other chemical elements may be present – ammonia vapour, for example – that could irritate nasal passages.

14

4 Do not eat, drink or smoke in the dyeing area. This is standard safety practice, not something exclusive to dyeing. Chemicals are not made to eat and care should be taken to prevent them from being transferred to the mouth by contact with food or utensils, or the moist end of a cigarette. Additionally, particles of a chemical dye making contact with the hot end of a cigarette could be decomposed by the heat to give off noxious substances.

5 Equipment must be reserved for use with dyes and nothing else. Pots, pans, jugs, etc could be contaminated by contact with other materials, and the colour of the dyes could then be adversely affected. It is also possible, though perhaps unlikely, that unwanted chemical reactions might occur. Conversely, equipment used for other purposes, and especially in connection with food, must never be used for dyeing.

If containers or equipment are being reused for dyeing, they should be thoroughly washed out and any existing labels removed or obliterated; old cooking utensils being reused should be marked clearly to indicate their new purpose. Check that the material from which such second-hand equipment is made is suitable for its intended use in dyeing: will it withstand acids, alkalis, boiling water? Will it react with any chemicals being used? Is it stable and unlikely to topple over? And so on.

6 Use suitable containers for dyes and chemicals. In the first place, all containers should be labelled to indicate clearly what is inside them. If the contents could be harmful, the label must indicate the fact.

Choose containers that can be closed securely so that no spillage will occur if they are overturned. If the contents are likely to contribute to a fire, keep them in a fire-resistant container such as a tin, lined with a plastic bag and having a secure lid.

Finally, keep all containers securely closed except when actually withdrawing or adding to the contents.

7 Store dyes and chemicals in a suitable place. The place chosen should be secure from tampering, especially by children. A lockable cupboard or chest is strongly advocated in family environments.

The location of the store should be cool and dry to safeguard containers and contents from overheating and damp.

8 Pay attention to personal hygiene. Always wash in warm soapy water after using dyes, as much for cleanliness as for health. Attention to hands and face should normally be all that is necessary, but if there has been an accident causing significant amounts of powder or liquid to be spilled or splashed, remove contaminated clothing for laundering and wash all exposed skin areas. Use a brush to clean under finger nails and cuticles.

In the event of dye liquids or chemicals being splashed in the eyes, irrigate them with clean water for at least 5 minutes. Qualified medical attention should then be obtained as necessary. If medical help is sought, remember to name the chemical causing the problem.

9 When mixing acids or caustic with water, always add the chemical to the water and never the other way round. When some acids and dry alkalis get wet they generate heat very rapidly. If water is incorrectly being added to such materials, the rapid generation of heat will cause the first few drops of water to boil, and the ensuing spitting and spurting can forcibly eject particles of the hot chemical. In a glass or similar container this could be especially dangerous.

The correct procedure of adding the chemicals to the water does not prevent heat being generated, but it does provide a relatively large volume of liquid in which the heat can be absorbed safely.

10 In domestic surroundings all working surfaces should be covered before dyeing begins. A few layers of newspaper are suitable because their absorbancy will prevent spillages from travelling. After dyeing, these coverings should be carefully folded together and discarded, and the surfaces beneath wiped clean with a damp cloth.

2
FIBRES AND YARNS

In this chapter we consider fibres solely in relation to dyes. If they are to be coloured satisfactorily one must know which dyes to use; there is no single dye that will colour all fibres equally well so we must identify the fibre in order to choose the right dye. We also need to know what characteristics it has that might affect dyeing so we can select the best way of applying colour to it. This chapter is all about such things.

Only the fibres most likely to be dyed are examined; others that are normally used in their natural colour – camel, for example, or yak – are not discussed. Charts at the end of the chapter present all the information in tabular form.

Types of fibre

A fibre is 'any fine thread-like object, of animal, vegetable or mineral origin, natural or synthetic'. There are two forms – filament and staple. A filament is a fibre of continuous length, either man-made or natural (the only natural filament is silk); a staple is a fibre of limited length that has to be twisted with other fibres before it can be made into a yarn. Filaments are sometimes cut into staple lengths and then spun on their own or in mixtures with other staples; this makes identification difficult.

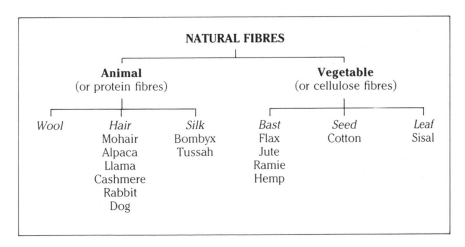

Fig 1 *Family tree: natural fibres*

Fibres are also classified by origin as natural, or man-made. The natural fibres are animal, vegetable and mineral, but in practice mineral fibres can be discounted as the only example of any consequence is asbestos, which is now disfavoured on safety grounds and was seldom if ever used by craftworkers, anyway. Man-made fibres are of two types, the regenerated or cellulosic, and the synthetic.

Fig 2 *Family tree:*
man-made fibres

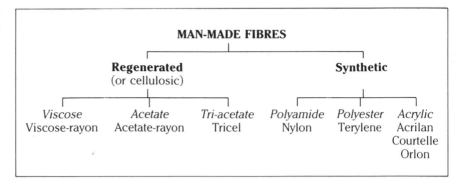

There are many sub-varieties of each main fibre type, and the charts at Fig 1 and 2 show those of significance in dyeing.

Animal
fibres
Wool

There are many different breeds of sheep, with wool varying in length, fineness, crimp (wavyness), quality and colour; it varies from fine, soft merino used in the best botany wools, to coarse Scottish blackface, mainly used for carpets and rough tweeds.

Like all the animal group, wool is a protein fibre composed of many cells. At its surface these appear as flattened scales, overlapping in the same direction towards the tip of the fibre; this layer is called the epidermis. The main part of the structure is the cortex, made up of long, spindle-shaped cells enclosing the medulla, a core of air-filled capillaries (see Chapter 4, 'Wetting'). The medulla is almost non-existent in very fine wools such as merino.

The outer scales are responsible for some of the unique characteristics of wool. They create pockets of air that act as heat insulators and make wool a warm fibre; when it is spun, they interlock to produce a strong, elastic yarn. Interlocking also occurs during felting as the fibres shrink and become inelastic; the scales are drawn together but this time they cannot move apart.

Sheep are usually shorn once a year, although some rare breeds are plucked. Fleeces vary in weight from 1 to 6kg (2 to 13lb) and the staple – the name for a lock of wool from the fleece – can be anything from 4 to 40cm (1½ to 16in). After grading and sorting, the wool used in industry is scoured or washed to remove grease and impurities, before being spun; hand-spinners and dyers have to do this for themselves.

Wool fibres are prepared for spinning by either of two processes, the choice between them depending on the type of fleece and the purpose for which the yarn is intended. Short-staple wool is passed over rollers with wire teeth which draw all the fibres into an orderly arrangement; the same action is performed by hand-carders in craftwork. It is then spun into light, bulky 'woollen' yarn.

Fibres of the longer wools are first carded, then combed into alignment and to remove any short lengths (called 'noils'), and finally drawn out for spinning. The yarn resulting from this process is much stronger, smoother and more lustrous, and is called 'worsted'.

Most tapestry yarns are worsted spun and have more lustre than woollen spun botany and other knitting yarns (see Chapter 3, 'Colour and Texture'). They will thus reflect light and appear to be brighter in colour when dyed. Similarly, a Wensleydale fleece which is smooth and naturally lustrous will produce brighter colours than the same dyes on, say, a merino or southdown which is soft and woolly.

Alkali damages wool and should never be left in the fibre; if it has to be used in a dyeing process it should be neutralised with a weak acid during the rinsing sequence. Weak acids, on the other hand, do not harm the fibre and are used with the type of dyes mostly applied to wool – the acid group (see Chapter 5).

Wool takes dyes very well to produce even colours on yarn, but sometimes a variable tone effect on fleece. This is because the tips of the fibre get damaged when a sheep scratches itself against a post or lies on hard ground; the epidermis is abraded and the exposed parts of the medulla take dye very much more strongly than the rest and will appear darker in consequence. The resulting two-tone effect can produce a more lively colour when spun, and is one reason why it is sometimes preferable to dye in the fleece rather than in the yarn.

Silk Silk was cultivated in China as long ago as 2600BC, and is the most luxurious of all textile fibres and the only example of a natural filament. It is renowned for its lustre and brilliant colours when dyed, and size for size it is stronger than steel but elastic and absorbent. It is an important material in fashion fabrics, particularly designer dress-wear, and is sometimes blended with soft matt hair fibres, such as alpaca, to add lustre.

There are two main varieties of silk – bombyx and tussah. Bombyx silk is produced by the *Bombyx mori* silkworm which is cultivated on silk farms. Its main diet is mulberry leaves which have to be gathered daily, and it produces the best white filament.

Tussah silk is produced by wild silkworms of several varieties, typically *Antphereas mylitta*, which feed on oak leaves. Their silk is coarser but stronger than bombyx silk, and coloured creamy or brown from the tannin in their diet.

In both cases the caterpillar spins a cocoon when it has grown to about 7cm (3in) long, extruding two filaments which it cements together with a gum called sericin. About ten days after pupating, the wild silk moths hatch and eat their way out of the cocoons, thus damaging the silk filament. When it is spun this damage may appear as tiny slubs, and the fibre is usually cut and carded and then processed into a spun-silk yarn.

The same damage would occur with cultivated silkworms if they were allowed to hatch, but to preserve the filament unbroken the cocoons are steamed after eight days to stifle the grub inside. They are then softened in hot water to release the gum so that the silk filament can be wound off. Normally, filaments from a number of cocoons are reeled off together for spinning into a multi-filament yarn.

Silk dyes very readily with both wool and cotton dyes (see Chapters 5 and 7). Before dyeing it is sometimes necessary to remove any remaining gum to avoid uneven dyeing (see Chapter 4, 'Fibre Preparation').

Mohair Mohair comes from the angora goat – a native of Turkey but also farmed in the USA and Africa, and experimentally in Australia. It is the most important of the hair fibres, being white, lustrous, very soft, smooth and silky.

The goats are shorn once or twice a year and produce a fibre with a staple length of 15–30cm (6–12in). It closely resembles wool when seen under a microscope, although it has fewer scales and thus does not have the same tendency to felt; its fibre is also less liable to shrink.

Mohair is absorbent and takes dye extremely well, both as a fibre and when spun into a yarn; the same acid dyes are used as with wool. It can be brushed after spinning and weaving to produce a soft, fluffy appearance, but is nevertheless a very strong and hard-wearing fibre.

Alpaca The alpaca is a South American camel belonging to the llama family, and is kept as a domestic animal in Bolivia and Peru. It is shorn once a year, producing a fleece of about 30cm (12in) in length. The hair is lustrous and silky, and can be coloured brown, tan, grey, fawn or white – all these colours sometimes appearing on the one animal. It is quite strong, does not shrink, and the white and light colours can be dyed as easily as wool, although it is normal to leave them in their very attractive natural state.

Llama The llama is a very similar animal to the alpaca, both in appearance and colour, but having slightly coarser hair. It is mainly used as a beast of burden. Its fibre is a poorer quality than alpaca, being less strong and silky; the lighter colours can be dyed quite successfully with the acid dyes used for wool.

Cashmere This is a really luxurious fibre, produced by the cashmere goat that is native to Kashmir in Northern India, Tibet and Outer Mongolia. The hair is about 1–8cm (½–3in) long and is combed or plucked from the animal, the wiry outer or 'guard' hairs being then separated from the soft under-down. Only 100g (3–4oz) or so is obtained from each animal; it is very fine and silky, felts fairly easily, and can be dyed by the same methods and with the same dyes as wool, if care is taken.

Angora rabbit Fur from the angora rabbit is plucked or clipped, with 350g (12oz) on average being produced each year. It varies from 2 to 10cm (1 to 4in) in length and is very fine, light and silky. In spinning it is very often mixed with wool to produce a more bouncy yarn, while still retaining the fluffy appearance of the fibre. Angora may be dyed easily, but care must be taken not to let it felt; it is helpful to place it loosely in a bag made from muslin or nylon (old stockings or tights are ideal).

Dog The hair from the soft undercoat of dogs such as samoyed, husky, sheltie, etc is fine, soft and slippery, and is becoming a very popular fibre in hand-spinning, knitting and crocheting. It dyes easily with wool dyes (the acid group) but will felt unless particular care is taken. Placing it in a bag, as suggested for rabbit hair, may be helpful.

Cotton is the most widely used of all the textile fibres. It comes from the *Gossypium* plant – a member of the mallow family – which grows in hot countries, reaching a height of 120–150cm (4–6ft). When the flowers die, a seed pod or boll begins to grow and, after about seven weeks, it bursts, showing the fluffy cotton fibres inside. These are picked by hand or machine, and undergo several different processes before being ready for use.

Vegetable fibres
Cotton

Cotton is graded according to its fineness and length; the top quality with a staple of up to 5½cm (2¼in) is Sea Island cotton grown in the West Indies. The next best come from Egypt and the USA, while cotton from India and China is much shorter and coarser. The fibre grows as a hollow tube, but when it is picked and dried it twists and the tube collapses; under a microscope it looks rather like twisted ribbon.

Cotton is strong, readily absorbs moisture, and increases in strength when wet. It resists alkalis so it can be bleached, but it can be damaged by strong acids. It takes dye well, although not as easily as wool and silk because its 'woody' texture has to be broken down to allow the dye to enter.

Mercerised cotton is treated with caustic soda under tension, which causes the flattened fibre to swell and regain its original tubular form. It becomes more reflective in consequence, and its lustre and affinity for dyestuffs are increased; it also becomes even stronger. Mercerised yarn has a much brighter appearance when dyed than ordinary cotton.

Direct dyes (see Chapter 6) were originally developed for cotton, and have been supplemented in time by the reactive and vat types (see Chapters 7 and 8).

Possibly the oldest of the textile plant fibres, flax comes from the woody stem of the flax plant, *Linum usistatissimum*, tall and spiky with blue flowers, and growing to a height of about 1m (3–4ft). The plants are spaced very close together and are harvested by being pulled up by the roots. The stems are rotted, or 'retted', in water, after which the fibres are separated and eventually combed to remove the shorter 'tow' flax from the silky line flax which is used in spinning.

Flax (linen)

After flax fibres are spun into yarn they are called linen, which is also the name of the cloth woven from the yarn. Flax is a very strong fibre, and another of the few that are stronger when wet; its natural sheen makes it attractive for weaving and embroidery. Linen used to be bleached out of doors by exposure to sunlight, but nowadays alkalis are used for the process. This makes the yarn easier to dye, although the fibre is not particularly receptive – it is difficult for dyes to penetrate the closely packed molecules of the woody material and uneven colouring frequently results.

Jute is a bast fibre, mostly grown in India and Pakistan; it comes from the stem of the *Corchorus* plant, which reaches a height of 2½–5m (8–15ft), but the fibres are only 15–30cm (6–12in) long. They are processed in the same way as flax, the plant being cut during harvesting instead of being pulled up. Jute is a lustrous brownish fibre, and while the weakest of the bast fibres with little elasticity, it is still stronger than cotton.

Jute

Jute is normally used in its natural state, but it takes dye very well and is often employed by textile artists in the creation of large hangings; however, colours tend to fade and are best kept out of strong sunlight.

Sisal Sisal is obtained from the leaf of the *Agave sisalana* that grows in Central America, reaching a height of 6m (20ft). The fibres themselves are about 1–2m (3–6ft) long and are extracted by scraping away the fleshy parts of the leaf. They are stiff, white, lustrous and very strong, being used mainly for ropes and cordage, mattings and rugs.

Sisal can be spun fairly easily if it is kept damp, but as with jute, it is mostly used by craftworkers in three-dimensional hangings. It can be dyed easily with cotton dyes, producing brilliant colours for a period, but they tend to fade in time – a point that should be borne in mind.

Ramie Ramie is an underrated fibre in craftwork. It is lustrous, silky, very fine, strong, resistant to acids and alkalis, and washing and bleaching as well. It has been found in ancient mummy wrappings, and comes from the *Boehmeria nivea* plant, otherwise known as China grass because it is largely grown in China; it is also cultivated in Japan, Russia, and parts of the USA and Europe.

Fibres are only 15cm (6in) long, which makes them very manageable for spinning. They are pulled from the stalk and retted in much the same way as flax, and have to be treated later by a chemical process to remove pectin. Ramie fibres dye easily, giving bright colours from any of the cellulosic dyes.

Hemp Hemp is obtained from the stalks of the plant *Cannabis sativa* or *Cannabis indica*, and is processed in the same way as flax. It is greyish-brown in colour and a very ancient fibre, originating in China but now grown in Russia, China and Japan. It reaches a height of about 3m (10ft).

Hemp is the strongest of all the textile fibres and can vary in quality from fine to coarse. It is absorbent, fairly easy to dye, but for even results the alkali in the dyebath needs to be increased.

Man-made fibres Man-made fibres divide into two main groups – those that are regenerated from wood cellulose, and the synthetics made from chemical substances called polymers.

While man-made fibres are initially extruded, some of them are immediately chopped into staple lengths to be blended with other fibres, or used as spun staple yarns. Very many filament and staple yarns are used in textiles under such brand names as Orlon, Trevira, Teklan, etc, but only those likely to be used by craftworkers as yarn or fibre will be described in this chapter.

Regenerated fibres
Viscose Viscose rayon was the first man-made fibre, being introduced in 1905. It is made by reacting wood pulp with caustic soda and then extruding the result as a continuous filament which may be chopped into staple form for spinning. It is absorbent and widely used in textile applications, but fairly weak and at its best when blended with other fibres. Common brand names

are Evlan, Sarille, and Viloft – a new tubular form with extra absorbency.

As viscose is made from cellulose it readily dyes with conventional cotton dyes.

Acetate rayon is also made from wood pulp, but this time by an acid process introduced around 1920 in which acetic and sulphuric acids are used to dissolve the cellulose. The fibre that eventually results is extruded and spun as before.

Acetate

Acetate rayon is soft to the touch and drapes like silk, and resists stains. It cannot be dyed satisfactorily with the usual cotton or wool dyes, and a special type – disperse dye – was developed to colour it. The commonest brand name is Dicel.

The manufacture of tri-acetate rayon is similar to that of acetate, but a different solvent is used. The fibre may be spun as a filament or produced in staple form. It is not absorbent and does not shrink or stretch, and it may be blended with other fibres for use in knitting yarns. Dispersé dyes are used to colour it.

Tri-acetate

The most common brand names are Tricel (British), and Arnel (American).

Nylon was developed in the USA in 1934 from a mixture of coal and petroleum; after further processing it was then extruded as a filament. Originally it was used in textiles on its own, and its quick-drying and non-iron properties were attractive, but it turned out to be uncomfortable in garments as it does not absorb moisture and feels clammy when damp. Nylon is very abrasion resistant and, when chopped into staple and blended with wool or cotton, it adds to the life of woven or knitted fabrics. It is often blended with wool in knitting yarns.

Synthetic fibres
Polyamides

Because its structure is similar to wool, it can readily be dyed with wool dyes and disperse dyes (see Chapters 5 and 9).

Terylene is the well-known polyester fibre and another petroleum derivative, this time being a combination of ethylene glycol and an acid. It is extruded as a continuous filament which is chopped into staple. Its manufacture is similar to nylon, but its molecules are very close together, making dye penetration difficult unless special techniques are used; medium colours can be obtained with disperse dyes.

Polyester

Polyester staple blends well with wool, cotton and viscose, and improves their wearing qualities; as a single filament it is used in curtain netting and furnishing fabrics. Typical brand names are Dacron, Diolen, Lirelle, Terlenka, Terylene and Trevira.

Acrylic fibres were first produced in 1946 and made from ammonia, propylene and oxygen; these were dissolved in a solvent to make them viscous, and then extruded through spinnarets before being solidified in air. The staple fibres are similar to wool, being soft and warm with good strength and absorbency.

Acrylic

23

Acrylics are used a great deal in knitting yarns, sometimes being blended with wool, nylon and cotton. Typical brand names are Acrilan, Orlon and Courtelle; they may be dyed successfully with disperse dyes.

Fibre identification

One must know the identity of a fibre in order to select an appropriate dye to colour it. Yarns may contain a single fibre, eg wool, or they may be a mixture of fibres, eg wool/acrylic/nylon. There are several methods of identification available to craftworkers. Feeling the fibre and looking at it closely will indicate something of its type, while a simple burning test should reveal the group to which it belongs. Tests of this nature are described below, and charts at the end of the chapter summarise the main characteristics to be noted.

Examining the fibre

If the fibre is in yarn form, cut off about 30cm (12in), carefully untwist the ply and examine it to see if more than one type of fibre is present (a magnifying glass is useful and a dark, dull background helps if the fibre is white or light-coloured).

If loose fibre is to be examined, merely pull out a few strands and examine these.

Carefully separate a few strands to see if they are in staple or filament form. If they are staple fibres, note the length and the amount of crimp present. Note the brightness and lustre.

Test for strength and elasticity. Is the fibre elastic or brittle? Is it easy to break or does it need reasonable force? Wet the fibre and see if the previous observations are still true or if the characteristics of the fibre have changed.

Examine the fibre for smoothness and slipperiness between the fingers.

It may be that by consulting the fibres chart with the results of these tests it is immediately possible to reach a decision regarding the sample. If not, the burning test may be decisive.

Burning test

To conduct this safely, the following equipment is recommended: a heat-proof tray or plate over which to conduct the tests; a candle, in a holder if possible, to provide the source of flame; tweezers, to grasp the sample; a container of water, in case of accidents.

Remove a bundle of fibres from the sample, twist them together and hold them by one end in the tweezers. Move them slowly towards the flame, noting their reaction to heat. Do they shrink away from it, or soften and droop, or simply melt?

Now advance the sample into the flame. Does it burn rapidly or merely smoulder? Does it produce smoke, and if so, of what colour? Does it make any noise as it burns? Is there any smell and if so, what is it like?

Now withdraw the sample from the flame. Does it remain alight or is it self-extinguishing? Does it smoulder?

Examine the residue once it is extinguished. What colour is it and what does it look like? Is it a hard deposit or can it be crumbled between the fingers?

With the answers to these questions and the information gathered from the initial examination, it should be possible to identify the fibre by general type and thus decide what dye should be used for colouring it. However, there are two other tests that may be possible to confirm an identification.

Examine the fibre both lengthwise and in cross section. A magnification of at least 100–150 is desirable, and up to 300 is recommended. The appearance of the fibres is shown in Figs 3 and 4 which accompany the charts which follow.

Microscope

There are various stains that can be applied to fibres to help identify them. The collection referred to on the charts is produced by Shirley Developments in Manchester, and is known as the Shirlastain (see Information Sources suppliers, p129).

Staining test

When the fibre is wetted and immersed in the stain, a colour develops; the fibre is then washed, rinsed and examined. The colour is fairly individual to the fibre or fibre type, and provides yet another clue towards identity. Different stains have been developed for different groups of fibres, the one for most natural and man-made fibres being 'Shirlastain A'. The results from using this stain are noted on the fibres chart.

	FIBRE			FIBRE IDENTIFICATION					
					BURNING TEST				
Name	Type and form	Source	Appearance	Self-extinguishing or not	Near flame	In flame		Residue	Odou
Wool	Protein staple: 4–30cm (1½–12in)	Sheep	Soft, elastic, crimped, dull or lustrous	Self-extinguishing	Smoulders	Burns steadily, slight sizzle, blue/grey smoke		Crisp, black inflated bead, easily crushed	Burn hair
Mohair	Protein staple: 15–30cm (6–12in)	Angora goat	Strong, resilient, lustrous, medium crimp		As for wool				
Alpaca	Protein staple: 30cm (12in)	South American camel; llama family	Fine, soft, slight crimp, slight lustre, white or 'coloured', not much elasticity		As for wool				
Llama	Protein staple: approx 30cm (12in)	Llama family	Soft; not as fine as alpaca. Inelastic, slight lustre, white or 'coloured'		As for wool				
Cashmere	Protein staple: 1–8cm (9½–3in)	Tibetan or Kashmir goat	Very fine, light, silky, smooth		As for wool				
Angora	Protein staple: 2–10cm (1–4in)	Angora rabbit	Very soft, fine, silky, light		As for wool				
Samoyed, husky, etc	Protein staple: 2–8cm (1–3in)	Dog	Smooth, silky, no crimp. Fineness varies		As for wool				
Silk: bombyx (white)	Protein filament (sometimes cut)	Cultivated silkworm, *Bombyx mori*	Very fine, smooth, shiny, elastic	Self-extinguishing	Smoulders	Burns steadily; slight sizzle		Crisp, black, inflated mass	Burn hair
Silk: tussah	Protein filament (sometimes cut)	Wild silkworm, eg *Antheraes mylitta*	Not as fine as bombyx; pale brown, shiny		As above				

| FIBRE IDENTIFICATION | | STAINING | PROPERTIES AFFECTING DYEING | DYEING | | |
| MICROSCOPE | | | | | |
Length-wise	Cross-section			Types of Dye	Affinity
Scaly surface	Round or oval; hollow	Golden yellow	Absorbent; weaker when wet; shrinks and felts; dry heat damages; alkalis bad	All acid dyes; chrome; special reactive	Very good
Not as scaly as wool	Round or oval	Orange yellow	Very strong; will not shrink; alkalis bad	As for wool	Excellent
Fairly smooth	Round or oval	Pale yellow	Stronger than wool; does not shrink or felt; will not bleach	As for wool	Good
As above		Yellow	As above	As for wool	Good
As above		Golden yellow	As for wool; may felt and shrink	As for wool	Very good
Smooth	Round or oval	Pale yellow	As for wool; felts and mats very easily	As for wool	Good
As above		Lemon yellow	As above	As for wool	Good
Round and smooth	Triangular with round corners	Orange brown	Absorbent; strong; dry heat, strong alkali, bad	All acid dyes – levelling poor; reactive; direct; basic	Excellent
Flatter than bombyx	Slightly triangular	Chestnut brown	As above but stronger; more resist acids and alkalis	As above	Excellent

WOOL

MOHAIR

ALPACA

SILK

| | FIBRE | | | FIBRE IDENTIFICATION | | | | |
| | | | | BURNING TEST | | | | |
Name	Type and form	Source	Appearance	Self-extinguishing or not	Near flame	In flame	Residue	Odo
Cotton	Cellulosic staple: 2–5cm (½–2in)	*Gossypium*; cotton boll	White, soft, medium strength, dull	Not self-extinguishing	Scorches, catches fire	Burns quickly; yellow flame	Grey ash	Bur pap
Cotton (mercer-ised)	As above		White, silky, strong, shiny	As above			Black ash	Bur pap
Flax (linen)	Cellulosic staple: up to 50cm (20in) but can be cut	*Linum usistatissimum*; flax plant, stem	Lustrous, not elastic, strong, fawn or brown or bleached	Not self-extinguishing	Scorches, catches fire	Burns quickly; yellow flame	Smoulders; grey ash	Bur pap
Jute	Cellulosic staple: 15–30cm (6–12in)	*Corchorus*; jute plant, stem	Yellow-brown not very strong; hairy	Not self-extinguishing	Scorches, catches fire	Burns quickly; yellow flame	Smoulders; black ash	Bur pap
Sisal	Cellulosic staple: 1–2m (3–6ft)	*Agave sisalana*; sisal plant, leaf	Lustrous, very strong, whitish, coarse	Not self-extinguishing	Catches fire	Burns steadily; orange flame, blue smoke	White ash	Bur pap
Ramie	Cellulosic staple: 6–20cm (2½–8in)	*Boehmeria*; Chinese nettle or Chinese grass; stem	Fine, similar to linen	Not self-extinguishing	Catches fire	Burns steadily; orange flame; blue smoke	Black or grey ash	Bur pap
Hemp	Cellulosic staple: about 80cm (32in)	*Cannabis sativa* or *Cannabis indica* stem	Darkish in colour; stiff; lustrous and strong	Not self-extinguishing	Begins to burn	Burns steadily; yellow flame	White ash	Bur pap

FIBRE IDENTIFICATION		STAINING	PROPERTIES AFFECTING DYEING	DYEING	
MICROSCOPE					
Lengthwise	*Cross-section*			*Types of Dye*	*Affinity*
Flat, like twisted ribbon	Flat tube	Lilac	Moderately absorbent; resists alkalis	Reactive, hot and cold; direct; vat; azoic	Good
Smooth and round	Hollow tube	Purple	Absorbent; very strong	As above	Better than above
Jointed like bamboo	Hollow, irregular polygon	Dark purple, grey	Very strong, especially when wet; bleaches readily	As above, but difficult to dye evenly	Poor
Similar to flax, but more hairy	Hollow, irregular polygon	Golden brown	Weaker than flax; deteriorates with age	Reactive, hot and cold; direct; acid	Good, but may fade
As above		Golden brown	Very strong, quite resilient	Reactive, hot and cold; direct; vat; acid; azoic	Very good but apt to fade
Similar to flax, but smoother	Bean-shape; slit centre	Lavender	Very strong; does not shrink; OK acid and alkali; absorbent	As for cotton	Good
Similar to flax, but smoother	Irregular rounded polygon	Reddish grey	Similar to flax; very strong; poor elasticity; absorbent	Reactive; direct; vat; basic; azoic	Good

COTTON

FLAX

JUTE

RAMIE

| | FIBRE | | | FIBRE IDENTIFICATION | | | | | |
| | | | | | BURNING TEST | | | | |
Name	Type and form	Source	Appearance	Self-extinguishing or not	Near flame	In flame		Residue	Odou
Rayon	Filament or staple	Viscose: wood pulp* alkali	Resembles cotton	Not self-extinguishing	Burns	Burns quickly; yellow flame		Feathery ash	Burnt paper
Acetate rayon	Filament	Acetate: wood pulp* acid	Smooth and silk-like	Not self-extinguishing	Melts	Sputters and burns quickly		Irregular charred bead	Burnt paper vinega
Tricel Arnel	Filament then staple	Tri-acetate: wood pulp* acid	Smooth, soft and silk-like	Not self-extinguishing	Shrinks and fuses	Burns quickly, melts and drips		As above	As abo
Nylon	Filament or staple	Polyamide: coal and petroleum	Smooth and light	Self-extinguishing	Shrinks	Melts, drips and froths		Hard, greyish, fawn bead	Fresh celery
Terylene	Filament then staple	Polyester: petroleum and anti-freeze	Smooth	Self-extinguishing	Shrinks	Softens and melts; black smoke with fawn bead		Hard, irregular bead	–
Courtelle, Acrilan, Orlon	Staple	Acrylic: ammonia, propylene and oxygen	Soft and warm	Not self-extinguishing	Shrinks and melts	Sputters and burns rapidly		Hard, black, irregular bead	–

*Regenerated fibre

FIBRE IDENTIFICATION			PROPERTIES AFFECTING DYEING	DYEING		
MICROSCOPE		STAINING TEST				
Lengthwise	Cross-section	(cold)		Types of Dye	Affinity	
Smooth, with lines	Irregular	Pink	Not strong, weaker when wet; inelastic	Reactive, direct, vat, azoic	Good	VISCOSE RAYON
Smooth	Irregular	Bright, greenish-yellow	Not strong; absorbent	Disperse	Fairly good	ACETATE RAYON
Smooth	Irregular, oval	Unstained	Not strong; not absorbent	Disperse	Fairly good	TRI-ACETATE (TRICEL)
Smooth	Round	Dull yellow	Strong, elastic; not very absorbent	Acid, disperse, reactive	Good	POLYAMIDE (NYLON)
Smooth	Round	Unstained	Strong, elastic	Disperse	Needs high temperatures or pale	POLYESTER (TERYLENE)
Smooth	Dumb-bell shaped (Orlon)	Acrilan: pink/grey; others: unstained	Strong, absorbent	Disperse, basic	Good	ACRYLIC (ORLON)

31

3
COLOUR THEORY

Colour is what this book is all about: dyes are colour; paints are colour; colour surrounds us everywhere. It is the element that brings vitality to our environment and stimulates our moods and attitudes. Yellow invigorates with all the freshness of a spring morning; orange suggests brightness and warmth; blue is cool and serene, while green calms us and puts us in harmony with our surroundings; purple is rich and regal and inspires reverence, but aggressive red is a dominating force that demands attention and will not let us rest or relax.

We subconsciously respond to these stimulations – a fact used by interior designers, advertising and publicity agencies, fashion and fabric artists who all use colour to produce the responses they want in us. The subject of colour is immensely wide, and in this book we deal with it very briefly to explain how colours blend and work together so that dyes may be chosen and used successfully. Students wishing to pursue the subject more deeply are advised to consult the many excellent books on colour technology, some of which are listed in the Bibliography and Further Reading sections at the end of this book.

Colour in light

In 1676 Sir Isaac Newton is said to have performed his classic experiment of passing daylight through a prism to break it down into its components of red, orange, yellow, green, blue, indigo and violet – immortalised in the classroom mnemonic, 'Richard Of York Gave Battle In Vain'. Later he passed the same colours through another, inverted prism and recombined them to produce white light once more. These simple experiments are the basis for our understanding of colour as it appears in the form of light – which we will call 'optical colour'.

The most obvious source of light is natural daylight, also called white light because this is how it normally appears. It is a form of radiation that begins in the sun and travels outwards through space as waves of energy. The distance between one wave and the next – the wavelength – varies enormously and gives rise to many different forms of natural radiation – gamma rays, X-rays, radio waves, and so on. Light waves which are visible – the 'visible wavelengths' – occupy a tiny part of this great band of energy, and even within this tiny section there are individual wavelengths, each associated with a particular colour.

The visible waveband extends from the threshold of the ultraviolet region (the shortest of the wavelengths) to the beginnings of the infra-red (the

Plate 1 (Top) *Dye colour circle, showing acid milling dyes applied to wool in different strengths and mixtures.* (Bottom) *The same dyes have been used as paints in colour sampling*

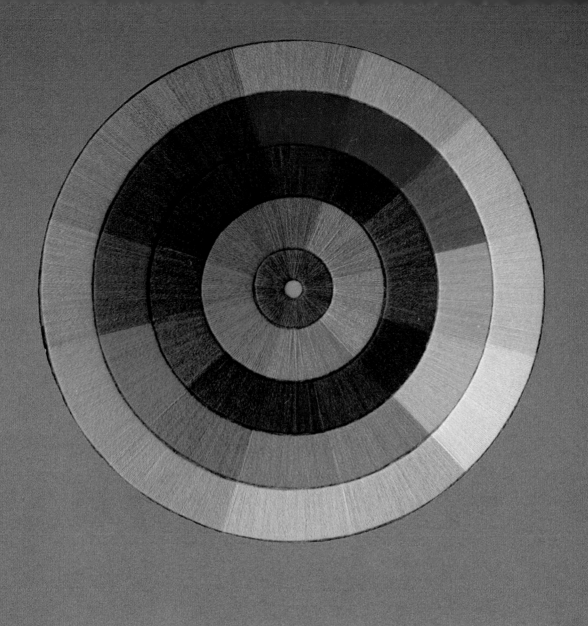

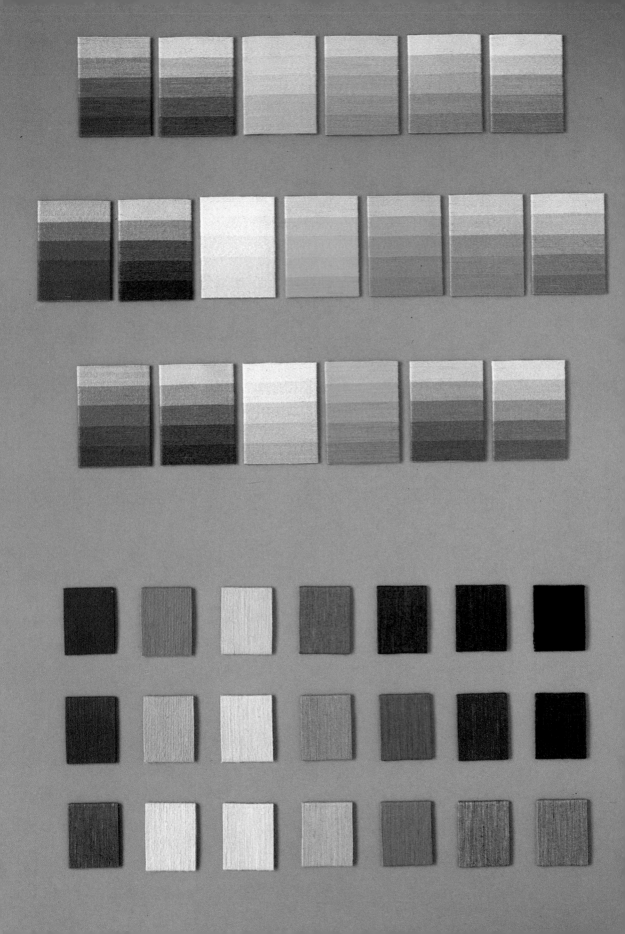

longest of them). In between these extremes each colour has its own wavelength, gradually getting shorter as we move from red to violet through the spectrum. There are probably around two hundred or so hues when one takes into account those that are formed where the seven main colours mix and blend.

When light of a particular wavelength reaches our eyes it produces a unique effect which we can distinguish from similar effects caused by light of other wavelengths. In childhood we learn to give names to these sensations and can describe them in terms of colour; one we call 'blue', another 'green', and so on. In this way we are able to specify the colours and mixtures of colours that we see.

Having shown that if the seven main colours of the spectrum are combined they will produce white light, Newton went on to demonstrate that if one or more of those colours was missing, the light that resulted would not be white but coloured, its hue varying according to the colours remaining in the mixture. Thus, green light + blue light − greenish/blue (cyan); blue light + red = reddish/purple (magenta); and green light + red = yellow. The latter may be surprising until one examines Fig 5 which shows the wavelengths involved. These effects may readily be observed in the mixtures of lights used for stage illumination.

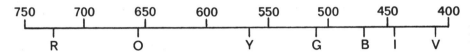

Fig 5 *The average wavelengths of colour*

There are three colours, however, that cannot be made by mixing light − red, blue and green. Because of this special characteristic they are known as the 'primary colours of light', or 'optical primaries' for short. They have another feature as well: they each contain about a third of all the visible wavelengths so that between them they span roughly the whole of the spectrum (see Fig 5). Newton showed that if all the colours of the spectrum were combined, the result would be white light; thus, a combination of red, blue and green will also produce white light if they are mixed in equal quantities. If the proportions are not equal, the light will be coloured instead of white, according to the balance between the three colours. By deliberately varying this balance it is possible to make all of the very many colours contained in the spectrum.

This is the principle on which colour television is based. The inside of the screen is covered with a pattern of triple phosphors, each producing the primaries, red, blue and green. Signals from the television transmitter energise these phosphors in varying proportions, and thus produce all the colours we see.

Since optical colours are made by adding the primaries together in varying amounts, the process is called 'additive mixing'; the colours of light are

Plate 2 (Top) *Reactive dyes on mercerised cotton showing colours at different strengths.* (Bottom) *Direct dyes on cotton showing various colours and strengths* superimposed on each other. This is the reverse of what happens with pigments and dyes where colours are absorbed or 'subtracted' from the total.

We noted that when the optical primaries were mixed together in pairs in equal amounts, they produced cyan, magenta and yellow. These are called 'optical secondaries' because they are made by adding together pairs of primaries. They have important characteristics as well which are most readily explained by reference to a diagram known as a colour circle, or wheel. The circle is divided into six equal segments and the primary colours are marked in alternate divisions as shown by the capital letters in Fig 6. Secondary colours are then indicated by small letters placed in the remaining segments between the parent primaries.

Fig 6 The optical colour circle

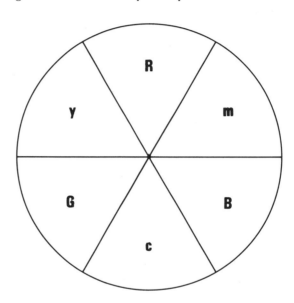

Examining this diagram we see that each secondary appears opposite a primary. Colours in this relationship are called 'complementary' colours because they add together or 'complement' each other to produce white light. For example, the secondary colour, magenta (little 'm' on the diagram) is a mixture of the primaries red and blue, which between them account for roughly two-thirds of the visible wavelengths; therefore, magenta must contain the same spread of wavelengths. The remaining third is contained in the other primary, green, which appears opposite magenta on the colour circle. Thus, magenta and green complement each other because when they are added in the correct proportions white light is formed. The same situation exists with red and cyan, and yellow and blue. Any secondary mixed with its complementary primary in the correct proportions will produce white light. Thus:

Green + magenta
Red + cyan ⎫ = white light
Blue + yellow ⎭

Complementary colours have another feature – they represent the greatest possible contrasts. Thus, cyan is the most strongly contrasting optical colour to red, and so on. The colour circle makes it easy to identify such contrasts.

We see the moon because it is illuminated by light from the sun, some of which is reflected down to earth; it is this reflected light we see – the moon emits none of its own. Exactly the same process enables us to see all the objects around us. Light falls on them and is reflected, and our view of the reflection tells us the shape and colour of the object.

Colour in pigments and dyes

The colour of this reflected light is affected by two things – the pigmentation of the surface from which it is reflected, and the characteristics of the light itself. It is easiest to consider these factors one by one, and to assume for the moment that we are dealing with daylight – white light.

The surface of almost all objects absorbs and retains some of the light falling upon it, and only a part is reflected for us to see. The colour of the object is dictated by the wavelengths contained in the reflected light. A simple example illustrates this. If daylight falls upon a red apple, pigments in the apple skin will absorb all the visible wavelengths except red; this colour is the only one reflected and thus we see the apple as red. Similarly, we see a lemon as yellow because its surface absorbs all the wavelengths except yellow; a plum looks purple because some of the red and blue wavelengths are reflected while all the others are absorbed.

Snow, on the other hand, absorbs virtually nothing and reflects back most of the white light falling upon it; thus we see it as white. A blackboard absorbs almost everything and reflects very little, so it shows no colour and produces the visual sensation we call black. Grey acts similarly but to a lesser extent; it absorbs all the wavelengths in the manner of black, but to a lesser extent so a little light is reflected to create the effect we call grey. In between these few examples are all the myriad combinations of absorption and reflection that create all the colours we see around us.

The colour we see is also affected by the nature of the light. White light contains all the visible wavelengths, but other forms of light may not. Sodium or mercury vapour lamps emit only a part of the visual spectrum, while tungsten filament and fluorescent lights contain all the wavelengths but in different proportions to white light. These differences affect the wavelengths that can be reflected and thus the colours of objects seen under those conditions.

Artificial pigments in paints and inks and dyes behave exactly like natural pigments, but with one important distinction – they are man-made to produce a particular effect. If the characteristics of a light source are known it is possible to make a pigment that will reflect any chosen wavelengths under those conditions. Generally, white light is assumed to be the source of illumination, but for some purposes – dyes for indoor colour film, for example – a different light source may form the basis for pigment design.

Another feature of pigments is that they produce colour in the opposite manner to light. When optical colours are added together the mixture becomes progressively lighter, eventually reaching white light when all the colours are present in the correct proportions. When pigment colours are added to each other they progressively absorb more and more light; by reflecting less they become steadily darker and eventually reach black. This process is called 'subtractive mixing' because wavelengths are progressively subtracted from the original white light, and it is an important point for dyers. Too many dyes mixed together will give muddy results. Note that subtractive mixing is the opposite of additive mixing by which optical colours are made.

In the eighteenth century a physicist named le Blon experimented with subtractive mixing techniques and discovered that while many pigment colours could be made by this method it was impossible to produce red, blue and yellow. Because of this he called them 'pigment primaries', and in pigment terms they occupy a similar place to optical primaries in their context.

Pigment primaries can be combined in pairs to form pigment secondaries; thus, red and yellow combine to absorb all the wavelengths except orange, which is thus the colour we see. Similarly, yellow and blue absorb all the wavelengths except green, and blue and red together reflect only violet. As with optical primaries and secondaries, these relationships can best be shown on a colour circle, but in this case it is slightly changed in layout. The next passage in this chapter deals more fully with the pigment colour circle.

A great many colours can be made by mixing pigment primaries, but if black is included in the group and if all the tonal values are well matched, the collection can produce just about all the known colours. This is an asset for artists or dyers working on a limited budget who do not wish to invest in an extensive palette; with just three properly matched hues plus black, it is possible to make most colours.

The pigment colour circle

The most useful layout is the twelve-segment diagram designed by Johannes Itten in the early nineteenth century. The three pigment primaries, red, yellow and blue, are located at equal distances apart with three blank segments between each of them, as shown by the capital letters in Fig 7. The pigment secondaries are marked in the centre of each blank set as indicated by the small letters, orange between red and yellow, green between yellow and blue, and violet between blue and red.

As with optical colours, complementaries are located opposite each other. Thus, the complementary of red is green; orange is the complementary of blue; and violet is the complementary of yellow. As before, these are the colours with the greatest contrast.

Because each secondary colour is composed of two primaries it has their combined absorption characteristics. When mixed with the remaining – and complementary – primary, it has the characteristics of all three primaries mixed together, ie virtually all light falling on the mixture is absorbed, producing black, grey or a darkish-brown, depending on the proportions of the mixture. This relationship is useful when mixing dyes. A small amount of its complementary will 'grey' or mute the main colour, and give a more vibrant effect than merely adding black.

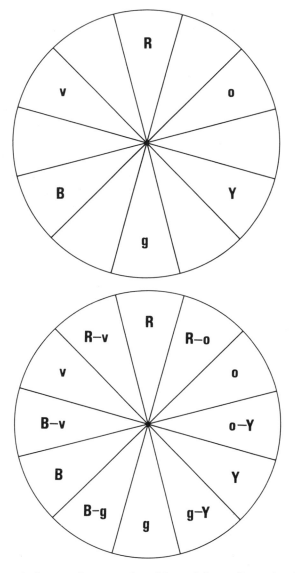

Fig 7 *The pigment colour circle, stage 1*

Fig 8 *The pigment colour circle, stage 2*

The colour circle can be completed by mixing adjacent primaries and secondaries to fill in the blank segments. Thus:

Red + orange = reddish/orange
Orange + yellow = orange/yellow
Yellow + green = green/yellow
Green + blue = blue/green
Blue + violet = blue/violet
Violet + red = red/violet

While the greatest contrast is represented by the colours opposite each other, those in adjacent or nearly adjacent segments represent harmonies. These are known as 'analagous' colours (analagous = similar, having some resemblance to). Thus orange, red/orange and red are all analagous colours; similarly blue, blue/violet and violet, or green, green/yellow and yellow.

Contrasts and harmonies can be identified very readily from a colour circle. The twelve-segment layout of Johannes Itten is sufficient to demonstrate the principle, but it can be enlarged to accommodate more segments and more colour mixtures, becoming a useful design tool for those who may not have an intuitive feel for colour and who need to sit down and plan harmonies and contrasts to achieve a satisfactory result. Students who plan to make their own circle might be interested in extending its usefulness by cutting a disc of the same diameter from a piece of card; the segments shown in Fig 9 are then marked and cut out to reveal analagous, complementary and monochromatic colours. By centering the disc over the colour circle and turning it as necessary, these relationships can immediately be identified.

Fig 9 The pigment colour circle overlay

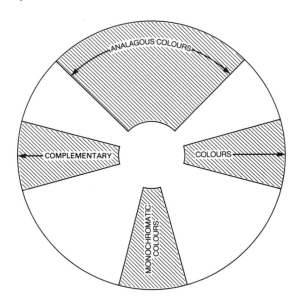

Tertiary colours are obtained by mixing pairs of secondaries, thus:

Orange + green = yellow ochre
Green + violet = olive
Violet + orange = russet

The relationships between primary, secondary and tertiary colours are shown in diagrammatic form in Fig 10. Each tertiary is composed of all three primaries in an unbalanced combination; russet, for example, is a mixture of orange and violet; orange is itself a combination of red and yellow, while violet is the product of blue and red. Russet is thus a combination of two of red, one of yellow, and one of blue. This is why red predominates in the tertiary colour, and why the combination of all three primaries produces a muted colour instead of black.

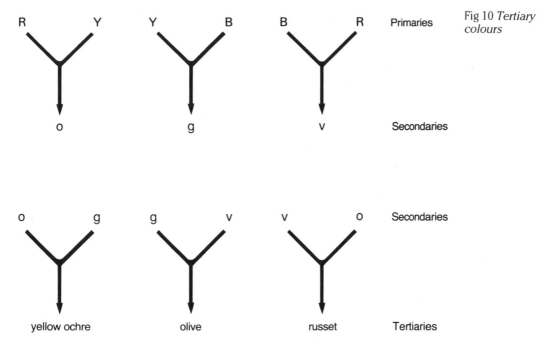

Fig 10 *Tertiary colours*

We do not always see colours as they really are. Their proximity to each other can alter their appearance; a monochromatic background can affect the response of our eyes, even lighting can affect the balance between colours. These phenomena are matters that should be considered when planning the use of colours, and as they are all connected with vision it is convenient to start at the eye and consider how it responds to colour. **Colour and vision**

Light entering the eye is focused on the retina where nerve cells respond and send appropriate information to the brain. These cells are of two types called rods and cones because of their shape when seen under a microscope, and there are several million of them. The rods are sensitive to light and dark and to differences in tone, but are not receptive to colour. The cones, which are more numerous, are colour sensitive and pass information to the brain which it decodes in terms of hue, tint and shade, etc.

It is believed that the cone cells are arranged in clusters of three, each cell being sensitive to one of the three optical primaries, red, green and blue. This is the arrangement duplicated on the screen of a colour television receiver. The three cells work together interpreting coloured light entering the eye according to the principle of additive mixing. If the eye sees white light all three cells are equally stimulated and their combined output to the brain signals 'white'; if the light is coloured, only the cells responsive to that colour will provide an output, while the others remain passive and at rest.

This concept of active and resting cells provides an explanation for some of the phenomena that occur in colour vision.

If one concentrates intently upon an area of a particular colour and then looks away to a differently coloured area, the image of the first may be seen for a short while superimposed on the second, but in the near-comple- **Colour phenomena** *After-image* mentary colour of the first. This is the phenomenon of 'after-image' and it can be produced by a simple experiment. Place a small bright blue object on a dark background and stare at it intently for about 20 seconds, then immediately transfer your gaze to a sheet of white paper. For a short while the shape of the blue object will be seen in its near-complementary colour of yellow-orange. The experiment can be repeated with other colours: concentration on a red object will produce a cyan after-image because the red cells will become fatigued and leave green and blue to provide the signal to the brain; likewise, a viewing of yellow will exhaust the red and green cells, leaving blue in the after-image.

Note that the after-images always appear in the near-complementary of the original colour. The significance that this effect has for a textile artist is in its relationship to another optical phenomenon called 'simultaneous contrast'.

Simultaneous contrast

The theory of simultaneous contrast was evolved by the French colourist Chevreul in 1839, following complaints about the quality of his dyes. He found that colours are affected by their neighbours and will change their appearance according to adjacent colours. When both are looked at simultaneously each imparts some of its complementary colour to the other through the after-image reaction, thus affecting the other's appearance.

This, too, can be demonstrated by a simple experiment. Cut a small square – say, about 35mm (1½in) – from a bright yellow card and place it alongside a similar square cut from a magenta card. Gaze at the pair of them for about 10–20 seconds and then check their apparent colours with the originals. The yellow will seem to have dulled and moved towards green, while the magenta will have acquired a violet tinge.

This happens because the complementary of one colour is carried across to the other. The complementary of magenta is green and when this is superimposed on the yellow it darkens it and gives it a greenish cast. Similarly, when the complementary of yellow – blue – is superimposed on magenta it causes a shift towards violet. The experiment can be repeated with other colours, for example, magenta and blue; in this case the blue darkens towards cyan while the magenta becomes paler.

It is important for craftworkers to appreciate this type of effect since it may influence the choice of colours to be used in a design. To avoid unwanted or unexpected changes in appearance, it is always best to select or match colours in the presence of any neighbouring colours, and not in isolation.

Successive contrast

Another effect is mentioned by William Watson in his book *Textile Design and Colour*. He notes that exhaustion of the cone cells of the eye causes a colour to appear duller the longer one looks at it. He illustrates this by referring to problems among some textile workers examining dyed cloth. Their appreciation of the tone of the colour gradually changed and it was found necessary to move them from time to time to a differently coloured fabric to avoid misjudgements due to this form of fatigue. The greatest amount of relief was found to come when the colour of the second cloth was near to the complementary of the first.

He also investigated the effect such fatigue might have on the next colour

FIRST COLOUR	COMPLEMENTARY	EFFECT ON NEXT COLOUR
Red	**Cyan**	**Blue** appears greener **Yellow** appears greener **Orange** appears yellower **Green** appears bluer
Blue	**Yellow**	**Red** appears orangey **Yellow** is more intense **Orange** appears yellower **Green** appears yellower
Green	**Magenta**	**Red** appears more violet **Yellow** appears more orange **Blue** appears more violet **Orange** appears redder

Fig 11 Successive contrast of colour

viewed, which he called 'the successive contrast of colour'. His results are presented in the above table; the complementary colour has been noted in each case to help explain the reason for the apparent colour shift.

Contrast of tone

If tints and shades of a colour are placed side by side, the lighter of an adjacent pair will appear to darken at its boundary with the darker tone, and the darker of the pair will appear to lighten at that boundary. The result can be a false impression of uneven colouring.

The effect is well represented in Plate 2 in the collection of reactive dye samples, especially in the reds and blues. If adjacent colours are masked off so that only a single tone is visible it will be seen to be evenly coloured; when the masks are removed the contrast of tone is again apparent.

Distance is significant when assessing colours. At long range they appear to merge into each other to give the impression of a single, composite blend. For example, if red and blue are alternated in stripes they will make a strong contrast at close range, but when seen from a distance they will blend into one another; the overall impression will be of magenta if the red stripes are wider than the blue, or of violet if the blue are wider than the red. The colour balance of a piece of work should always take into account the distance from which it will normally be seen and the effect this may have on the intended use of colours.

Colour and texture

If a piece of card is wrapped with a coarse yarn and illuminated from the side, each strand will be partly in light and partly in shadow. There will be an apparent change in tone as one views the wrapping from the illuminated or the shadow side. However, if the wrapping is made from a fine yarn the differences between light and shadow are much reduced because the yarn presents a more regular, even surface to the light; changes in tone are less apparent. This is one example of how texture can affect colour – the natural texture of the fibre, the texture it acquires when spun into a yarn, or the texture imparted by the processes of knitting, weaving, embroidering, and so on.

Smooth fibres like silk, nylon and other man-made filaments are substantially round in cross-section and have a smooth surface that reflects light. This gives them their natural brightness and lustre. Some man-made fibres, such as tri-lobal nylon, are given a special shape to have particular reflective qualities; others have so much natural brilliance that they appear harsh and are sometimes delustred to an acceptable level.

On the other hand, hairy fibres, like wool and mohair, and flattened fibres, like cotton and flax, all have an irregular surface that absorbs more light than the smooth fibres and thus appears dull and darker. An exception is mercerised cotton; the process to which it is subjected imparts an artificial lustre by swelling and rounding the otherwise flat fibre.

Lustre and brilliance are also affected by the way fibres are spun into a yarn. If a long-filament fibre such as silk is spun, or if a long-wool fleece is combed so that all the fibres lie alongside each other and is then worsted-spun, the surface of the resulting yarn will be more even than if the fibres had been carded before spinning. Because of the more orderly arrangement of the fibres these yarns will reflect more light and thus appear brighter. Carded fibres, which are usually of wool or hair, lie in all directions in a yarn, absorb more light and thus appear dull and darker.

The texture of a fibre and the fineness or coarseness of the yarn into which it is spun have a direct bearing on its overall colour effect. This is a point that spinners might wish to bear in mind when choosing and using raw materials for a particular project.

While this book does not cover fabric or cloth, it is relevant to consider briefly how the structure of a textile can affect the appearance of its colour. If fine lustrous yarns are laid evenly side by side to create an unbroken level surface, their colour will appear brighter than if coarse hairy yarns were used; in both cases the colour will be darkened if the surface of the fabric is uneven, as in a honeycomb weave, for example. Weavers and embroiderers will know that the smoother the surface of a textile, the brighter its colour appears to be.

Finally, 'finishing'. If a textile is brushed to bring all its fibres into an orderly arrangement it will reflect light better and appear brighter, but it will suffer at boundaries between different colours where there may be some diffusion and blending. If the surface is raised and cropped to a uniform nap, reflection will be reduced and colours will appear softer, but demarcations between them will be sharper.

4
GENERAL DYEING INFORMATION

Dyes are mixtures of finely ground chemicals that can be available as powders, granules or 'grains', and liquids. Mostly, craftspeople obtain them as powders. There is no single dye that will colour all types of fibre with equal effectiveness, or be suitable for all methods of dyeing; different dye compounds are made for different purposes.

Even though the dyes themselves may differ, however, there is a great deal of similarity in the ways they are used. In this chapter we have gathered together information on all the common procedures so they can be discussed and explained once only, thus avoiding frequent repetition in subsequent chapters.

The system of measurement used in dyeing, and in this book, is the metric system, although imperial equivalents are given where possible. There are two reasons for this choice. First, the metric system is the only one that allows the very small quantities used to be measured with sufficient accuracy. There is no problem in weighing 5g or even less; it would be difficult to weigh ⅙oz. Secondly, the equal relationship provided between weight and volume greatly simplifies the calculation of proportions, which are the basis of most dyeing calculations.

Equipment

Various items of equipment are needed in dyeing and should be provided exclusively for that purpose (see Chapter 1, 'Health and Safety'). The following list suggests those utensils and pieces of apparatus that might be regarded as essential.

Dyepots

Dyepots should be heatproof and non-reactive; dyebaths are often acidic and in contact with a reactive material – iron, for example – there might be an adverse effect on colour. Glass ovenware, enamelware or stainless steel are all suitable, with stainless steel perhaps the best of the three since it is inert, unbreakable and non-staining. However, it is also the most expensive.

Dyepots should be large enough to contain fibres at boiling or simmering temperatures without boiling over; this implies that they should not be more than about half full when containing the fibre and an appropriate quantity of water. They should have a base area large enough to cover a gas ring or electric hotplate used as a heat source; if the base is too small heat will be lost and it may be difficult to control the rate of temperature rise specified for a process.

Measures

For rough work, a calibrated jug or graduated beakers can be used, but for fine accurate measurements use a measuring glass, syringes, or 5, 10, and 20ml spoons and cups obtainable from chemists for use with medicines.

Weighing machines Most domestic weighing machines have 5g, or in the case of imperial units, ½oz, as their smallest weight, and this limits their usefulness, especially when mixing small amounts of dye. Slimmers' scales are a better alternative; they are available in two types – a sliding weight balance, and a spring balance. Either type can weigh down to 1g, and can be obtained from chemists or health shops. Electronic scales are more versatile and can weigh down to fractions of a gram or ounce, but are expensive and hardly justifiable unless a considerable amount of accurate weighing is likely.

Thermometer A thermometer is necessary to check the temperature of solutions and also to monitor the rate of temperature increase. A simple glass-rod type is sufficient; it should have a scale calibrated in both Centigrade and Fahrenheit, and show temperatures at least up to boiling point. Suitable models can be obtained cheaply from wine-makers suppliers and some chain-chemists. The Centigrade scale is best calibrated in single degrees; two-degree steps are sufficient for the Fahrenheit scale. An alternative is the kitchen 'sugar' thermometer, provided it is mounted on a heatproof, non-reactive backing. Floating thermometers are not suitable.

Stirring rods Stirring rods are used to mix solutions, to manipulate fibres in the dyebath and to transfer them from one container to another. They can be made at home quite cheaply from lengths of wooden dowelling, although they stain easily, may contaminate one dyebath with residues from another, and are difficult to clean. Glass or polypropylene rods are more expensive but do not stain and are easily cleaned.

Bowls and pots One can never have too many bowls and pots in which to mix dye solutions, hold dyes or other chemicals prior to use, carry wet fibres from one place to another, and so on. Spare dyepots and beakers can be used if available, but used yoghurt pots and margarine containers make excellent substitutes. Be careful that they will withstand the temperature of materials put in them.

Bottles Stock solutions of dye and other chemicals should be kept in bottles with sealing caps/stoppers. Plastic is safer than glass but should be robust enough not to split in use. Any old labels should be removed or obliterated and fresh ones applied to show clearly the nature of the contents (see Chapter 1, 'Health and Safety').

Safety equipment Rubber gloves are essential; the flock-lined type are easiest to put on and remove, and should be obtained in the gauntlet length if possible as this allows them to be pulled up over the cuffs and sleeves of jumpers and jerseys, and also allows access to fibres in a deep dyebath.

A simple facemask is advisable when handling dye powders in quantities and conditions under which significant amounts of dust might be liberated, and eye protection should be used when mixing solutions of caustic soda or acid (see Chapter 1, 'Health and Safety').

Notebook The elementary laboratory notebook is often overlooked. It is essential for the tidy recording of experiments, results, calculations, etc, so they are available for future reference. A pocket calculator is also useful for working out various dye calculations with a minimum chance of error and a maximum of convenience.

Yarn must be hanked before being subjected to any wet process or it is liable to tangle and become impossible to use. This is especially true of silk and hand-spun yarn. Wind it into a hank on a yarn-winder, niddy-noddy, or around a suitable book; tension should be as even as possible and not too tight or some parts of the yarn could become stretched. The two ends of the hank should be tied tightly together and then passed loosely around the hank before being tied again. The purpose of this is to show where the ends are, later on.

Fibre preparation
Hanking

Additional 'figure-of-eight' ties are required at intervals around the hank – three or four for cotton or commercial woollen yarn, but possibly more for hand-spun wool or silk (see Fig 12 for details). These ties should be secure enough to hold the hank in shape but not so tight that they impede the access of dye solutions – this could produce unwanted 'tie-dye' effects. The yarn used for ties is usually undyed cotton because it will not stain, and is strong and smooth.

Fig 12 *Figure-of-eight ties*

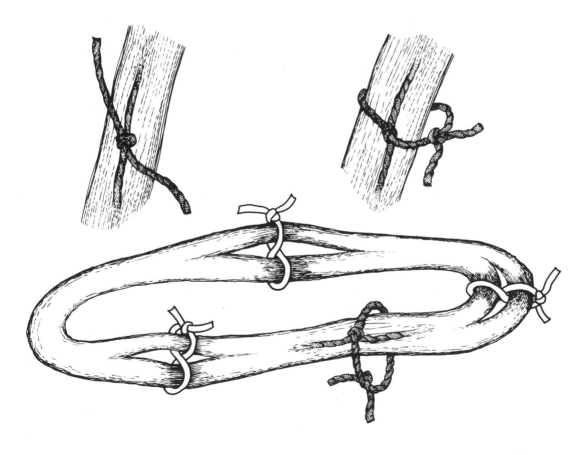

Scouring   Scouring is the process of thoroughly cleansing fibres to remove dirt, oil, grease and dressings so that dyes may combine with them effectively and evenly. If scouring is not undertaken there is a likelihood that patchy colouring will result; if there is any doubt regarding the cleanliness of fibre, it should be scoured. The process is simple but varies slightly with different types and forms of fibre.

Fleece and greasy woollen yarn will contain lanolin, dirt, and possibly other contamination as well, even water-soluble dyes used in stock marking and sheep breeding. All these are best dealt with by a two-part process.

1 Soak the fibres in a bath containing enough warm water (50°C (120°F)) to cover them, to which a little soap solution or detergent has been added at the rate of about 1.5ml per 100g of fibre. An ideal bath is one with a drain plug through which the water can be drained off without disturbing the fibres. Gently shake fleece to open it out, and carefully separate greasy yarn; they should be pressed below the surface of the bath to expel air, and left for at least an hour in the case of yarn, or overnight in the case of fleece. At the end of this period the dirty water should be run off without unduly disturbing the fibres; it is important to avoid any heavy handling as it could lead to felting.

2 The second part of the process – washing – can now be undertaken. Prepare a fresh bath, not more than hand-hot, and add a soap solution or good quality detergent; the amount is not critical but should be enough to create a good lather. Push the wool gently below the bubbles and leave it to soak for an hour or two, after which the bath is discarded as before. Rinse the wool in successive baths of water, all at the same hand-hot temperature, until the water runs clear. Remember to handle the fibres carefully.

3 Finally, remove excess water from the wool. A light spin for a few seconds is effective, fleece being enclosed in a suitable container – an old pillowcase, for example – before being placed in the spin-dryer. On no account should fibres be tumble-dried. After spinning, fleece should be gently teased out and either dyed straightaway or dried under good ventilation, away from direct heat and sunlight. Yarn, and especially hand-spun yarn, may benefit from a little light tension while drying.

Commercial yarn may or may not contain a light oil, depending upon whether it was obtained from a mill or bought from a retailer. If in doubt it should be washed, following the second and third parts of the previous process detailed for fleece. As with hand-spun yarn, drying under light tension may be beneficial.

Cotton and linen yarns are often 'finished' with dressings to improve their bulk, feel and whiteness; these finishes can impede dye penetration and should be removed. A different process is required from that suggested for wool.

The scouring bath should contain enough water to cover the fibres. Washing soda crystals are added at the rate of approximately 7g per litre of water (about 1oz per gallon). Detergent, as already described, should be added at a rate of 1.5ml per 100g of fibre (about ¼fl oz per lb). Start with the bath warm; stir in the soda and detergent to dissolve them and then add the fibres and leave them to soak for 20–30 minutes. Next, heat the bath and boil for at least an hour; boiling will not damage cotton or linen fibres but it will dislodge any finishes, and at the same time soften and open the fibres and partially break down their cellulose in readiness for even dyeing.

When boiling is completed, rinse the fibre thoroughly in baths of hot and then warm water, and either transfer it directly to a dyebath or dry it away from direct heat or sunlight. Hanked yarn may benefit from a little light tension while drying.

Silk fibre or 'reeled silk' is drawn straight from the cocoon; it does not need scouring but the natural gum it contains should be removed before dyeing. The two varieties of silk, bombyx and tussah, have slightly different chemical characteristics, and because of this slightly varying de-gumming recipes are necessary.

White silk (bombyx) is degummed in a bath containing approximately 20ml of a good quality soap solution per litre of water (about ½fl oz per pint), plus 10g (⅓oz) of washing soda crystals. Never use detergent with silk – it is too harsh.

Tussah silk is coarser and stronger, and for it a degumming bath may contain 30ml (¾oz) of soap solution and 20g (⅔oz) of soda.

In both cases, the bath is made with warm water in which the ingredients have been dissolved. The silk is added and the temperature carefully raised to not more than 80°C (180°F). If this level is exceeded, the lustre of the silk may be destroyed. Simmer for about 45 minutes and then thoroughly rinse the silk in warm water. Several rinsing baths will be necessary and the last but one should contain 30ml (¾oz) of white vinegar to neutralise any effects from the soda. The final bath removes the vinegar.

Spun silk is silk yarn, and possibly the form in which most craftworkers will encounter the fibre. Most, if not all, the natural gum will have been removed during the processes leading to spinning, so strong degumming baths are not necessary. For both varieties of spun silk, bombyx and tussah, the following procedure is sufficient to remove any residual gum.

Make the bath from warm water in which 15ml (about ½fl oz) of soap solution and 10g (about ½oz) of soda have been dissolved in a litre of water (about 1¾pt). Add the silk and simmer it for 30 minutes, taking care not to exceed 80°C (180°F). After this the yarn should be cooled and rinsed in warm water; several rinses will be necessary, the penultimate again containing 30ml of white vinegar per litre (about 2fl oz per pint).

After final rinsing, both silk fibre and spun silk should be transferred, either directly to a dyebath or to an area with good ventilation for drying away from direct heat and sunlight.

Wetting is the final stage in preparing fibres for dyeing; it is necessary to dispel air trapped in them so that dye can be taken up readily and evenly. *Wetting*

Cellulose and protein fibres contain long chains of molecules separated by small channels called capillaries; these are so small it is estimated that there may be ten million of them across the width of a single wool fibre.

49

Together they have an enormously large surface area – about a thousand times greater than the entire surface area of the outside. When a fibre of this type is dyed, very much more colour occupies the capillary spaces than attaches to the outer surface.

The capillary spaces of a dry fibre are filled with air which will block the entry of dye molecules and must be removed if effective dyeing is to be achieved. This is most easily accomplished by thoroughly wetting the fibre so that water drives out the air and can itself be replaced by dye liquor. However, water on its own is not very effective because its surface tension is too high, and must be reduced to allow penetration to all the capillaries.

Surface tension is lowered by adding a 'wetting agent' to the water. Wetting agents are a special type of detergent that create a very close contact between solids and liquids. In a wetting bath they reduce the surface tension of water by at least 50 per cent and allow it to make an intimate contact with the fibres and to penetrate into the capillary areas.

A wetting bath is prepared with enough water to cover the fibres being treated. A proprietary wetting agent, or for craftwork a good quality household detergent, is added at the rate of 2ml per litre of water. It is best not to exceed this amount, and if measurement is likely to be difficult it is better to err on the side of too little rather than too much.

The fibre is placed gently on the surface of the bath and will begin to sink as trapped air is displaced and buoyancy is lost. When it has completely submerged and lies at the bottom of the bath it will be reasonably wet, but may still contain some air, although not enough to allow it to float; to ensure that all the air has been driven out it is best to allow it to remain at the bottom of the bath for another 30 minutes.

Soaping   Soaping is a process similar to scouring but carried out after dyeing instead of before to remove unfixed dye from newly coloured fibres, especially cotton, linen, etc treated with reactive and direct dyes. If unfixed dye is not removed it may rub off later against neighbouring fabrics, stain during laundering, or run to areas where it is not wanted.

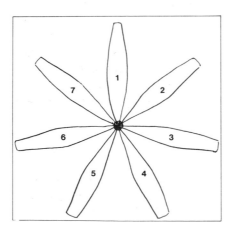

Plate 3 *Disperse dyes showing different colours on various knitting yarns in natural and man-made fibres. Key to outline chart: 1 100% wool; 2 acrylic/ nylon/wool mixture; 3 wool/acrylic mixture; 4 nylon/acrylic mixture; 5 100% acrylic; 6 cotton/ acrylic/polyester mixture; 7 wool/acrylic mixture in grey*

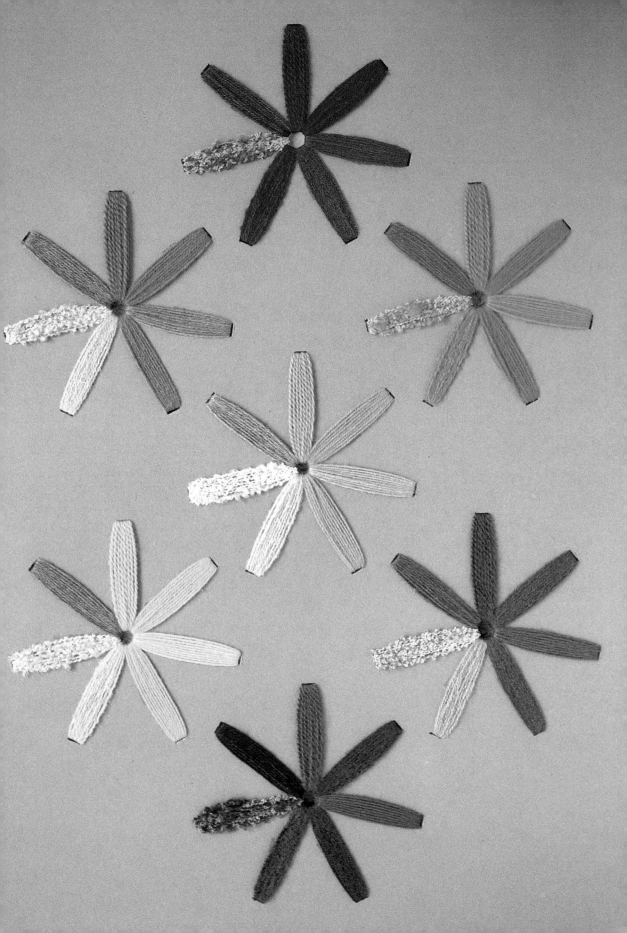

A soaping bath is made with sufficient water to cover the fibre, plus a little soap solution or detergent. Use only good quality, mild products, and add them at the rate of approximately 1.5–2ml per litre.

As the dyed fibres that require soaping are mainly cellulose, there is no problem in raising the temperature of the bath to boiling point and treating the fibres at that level for 10–15 minutes. After this, they are cooled and thoroughly rinsed before being dried. The procedures for using individual dyes will indicate when soaping is necessary, and any special requirements to be met.

Liquor ratio

The function of a dyebath is to carry dye and assistant chemicals to all parts of the fibres being coloured. The amount of water required can vary according to the type and method of dyeing, but in general there should not be too much so that part of the dye never reaches the fibre, nor too little so that part of the fibre is uncovered and never makes contact with the dye. Either of these two extremes can cause uneven colouring.

The relationship between water quantity and fibre is known as the 'liquor ratio', and is expressed as a proportion, eg LR = 20:1, meaning that 20 parts of water are required to 1 part of fibre, or in more practical terms, 20ml of water per gram of fibre.

It will be obvious that with a given amount of dye, its concentration in the dyebath will vary according to the amount of water present. Differing dyes and dyeing procedures sometimes require differing concentrations of dye in the bath, so it is not possible to suggest one common liquor ratio for all circumstances. Instead, the appropriate ratio is specified at the beginning of each of the dyeing procedures contained in later chapters. If a choice does exist, however, always use less water if possible to increase the dye concentration, but ensure that the fibres are covered adequately. Some

Plate 4 *Acid metal-complex dyes used on various yarns. Key to outline chart:* (Top), *showing colour on different yarns: 1a wool; b nylon; c mohair; d acrylic/nylon/wool mixture; e silk.* (Bottom), *showing rainbow-dyeing with the same dyes: 2 Wensleydale fleece coloured with the dyes in solution; 3 yarn spun from the above; 4 silk yarn dyed together with the fleece; 5 mohair yarn dyed together with the fleece; 6 grey roving dyed with dye powders*

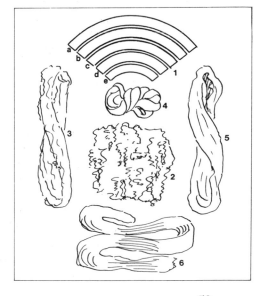

bulky fibres such as fleece or tops may require more water than an equivalent weight of yarn.

When dyeing at simmering or boiling temperatures, some of the dye liquor may be lost due to evaporation. This loss can be minimised by covering the dyepot, which will also reduce the escape of vapours into the atmosphere but may be inconvenient for temperature measurement and fibre manipulation. The alternative is to dye in an open dyepot and to make good liquor loss by adding boiling water as necessary.

Unless otherwise stated, soft water is preferred. In hard water areas a water softener should be used; domestic softeners such as Calgon are quite suitable, and should be used according to the manufacturer's instructions.

The acidity of the water may also be significant, especially when using the acid dyes. Acidity is indicated on a scale of values from 1 to 14, known as the pH scale. The mid-point is 7 where water is neutral – neither acid nor alkaline. As acidity increases, the scale values move from 7 towards 1; thus, a pH of 2 is strongly acid, but a value of, say, 6 is only weakly so. Similarly, the alkalinity of water is indicated on the range of values from 7 to 14, the higher numbers indicating the most strongly alkaline condition. The pH values required in dyeing are specified where appropriate in the dyeing procedures.

Acidity can be checked quite easily with test papers that are dipped in the dyebath and change colour to indicate the value of acidity or alkalinity. If the water is too acid it should be corrected by the careful addition of small amounts of precipitated chalk, available from chemists. If it is excessively alkaline, a similar application of vinegar can be made to obtain the required condition.

Dye solutions Commercial dyehouses use significant quantities of dyes which are measured out in appropriate amounts, mixed with water and dissolved as necessary, and then added directly to the dyeing machinery. This straight-forward approach is not convenient for craft dyers because the amounts of dye powder required are usually too small to be measured accurately. For example, a 100g (4oz) hank of fibre to be dyed to a standard 2 per cent depth of colour would require only 2g of dye; a 10g hank being dyed for colour sampling would need just 0.2g. These quantities are so small they are outside the range of most domestic weighing machines, and thus could cause measurement problems.

The difficulty is overcome by making dyes into solutions of a known strength which are used in proportionally larger amounts. This is the method followed in dyehouse laboratories which also use small amounts of dye in testing. Such mixtures are called 'stock solutions' and in most cases they can be made up when convenient for use later. Reactive dye powders are an exception, however; they begin to lose strength when they are mixed with water, and if full depth colours are required – as in shade matching, for example – they should be used as soon as possible after being mixed. They will still produce good and useful colours several months after being made into solution, but not to full strength.

A stock solution of dye can be made to any concentration, but the most convenient value for craftworkers is 1 per cent. This is very straightforward to make; 1 part of dye is mixed in 100 parts of water, or in more practical terms 1g of dye is dissolved in 100ml of water, or 5g in 500ml, and so on, keeping the ratio the same. For painting and spraying however, reactive dyes are usually made into a 5 per cent solution with the assistance of urea, and the addition of Manutex (see p57, 'Dyebath Assistants'). When making any dye solution, note that the dyes are not always manufactured to the same strength. The standard is 100 per cent, but sometimes dyes are produced stronger or weaker than this, frequently in the case of liquid forms (see Chapter 10, p89). If there is any doubt regarding the strength of a dye, refer to the maker's or supplier's literature.

The amount of stock solution to be made is a matter of choice, taking into account how well it will keep, how soon it is likely to be used, and how accurately the required amount of dye powder can be weighed. Accurate weighing is the most important consideration as a stock solution that is correctly blended will give dependable and repeatable results.

Dye powders do not dissolve in cold water, but they need to be mixed with a very small quantity of it to begin with to form a smooth paste. The dye is worked into the water until all lumps have been eliminated; this will help it to dissolve into a consistent and full strength solution later on.

Add boiling water to the pasted dye and stir until it is fully dissolved; about two-thirds of the final volume of liquid is sufficient. Once all the dye has been dissolved, add cold water to make up the balance of the solution.

Procedure for acid, direct and disperse dyes

Boiling water must not be used as it would damage or destroy the reactivity of these dyes, and thus their ability to combine with cellulose fibres. For cold-water dyes the water should not be hotter than room temperature – about 30°C (85°F) as a maximum; hot-water types should be dissolved in water that is just warm, say, 40°C (105°F). These are conservative figures; some brands of dye can withstand higher temperatures than this, but in a general note it is necessary to err on the side of safety. Manufacturer's instructions should always be followed if available.

Procedure for reactive dyes

Liquid dyes require slightly different treatment. Like powders and granules they may vary in strength according to type, or even according to colour within a type. It is important to establish the actual strength so that the correct amounts are used to make a 1 per cent stock solution. Deviation from standard strength is usually towards weaker, not stronger, dyes. As before, consult manufacturer's literature in cases of doubt.

Procedure for liquid dyes

Some liquid dyes may put down a sediment after prolonged storage; shake their containers to restore thorough mixing before any of the dye is measured out. Once the dye has been thoroughly mixed, the appropriate amount should be measured carefully in a measuring glass or with a syringe, and stirred into the correct volume of warm water to make the stock solution. The temperature of the water need not be above 45°C (115°F).

General   When stock solutions are sufficiently cool they should be bottled and labelled to show clearly the type of dye, its colour, solution strength and the date. Dating is particularly important with reactive dyes as it enables their age and condition to be assessed. Solutions should be stored in a secure place that is cool and dry (see Chapter 1 'Health and Safety'). Reactive dye solutions benefit from being refrigerated, but the feasibility of this must take into account security from tampering.

Dyebath   assistants   Dyebath assistants are a range of chemicals added to a dyebath to assist or moderate the dyeing process so that the best possible results can be obtained. Those of them likely to be used by craft dyers are presented in this section in alphabetical order.

Acids   Acids are used with acid dyes to increase the attraction between dye molecules and the fibre, thus promoting dyebath exhaustion. Different dyes require different strength acids, and sulphuric, formic and acetic are all used industrially. In craft dyeing it is possible to use dilute acetic acid in the form of ordinary vinegar, adjusting the quantity to compensate for the difference in strengths. Individual dyeing procedures contain details.

Acidic salts   With some types of dye that do not require a strong acid, an acidic salt such as ammonium acetate or ammonium sulphate is used instead. These salts acidify the dyebath slowly and progressively as temperature rises, assisting the even take-up of colour. They can be used dry and added to the dyebath at the beginning of the procedure, or made up in advance into a stock solution of known strength. The second alternative makes it easier to measure small quantities.

A 10 per cent solution is a convenient strength. It is made by dissolving 10g of the dry chemical in 100ml of boiling water, or 100g in a litre, or any other quantities provided the 10:100 ratio is maintained. Each 10ml of such a solution will contain 1g of the dry chemical.

Caustic soda (sodium hydroxide)   Caustic soda is used with vat dyes to provide the strongly alkaline conditions needed before the reduced dye will dissolve and be able to migrate to the fibre. Caustic soda can be used dry or dissolved into a solution. In the dry condition it tends to absorb moisture from the atmosphere and slowly turn into a paste; it is then difficult to weigh accurately. There is thus an advantage in making into a solution and keeping it in this form. Whether caustic soda is being used dry or as a solution, always be especially careful to add the caustic to liquid and never the other way round (see Chapter 1, 'Health and Safety').

A convenient strength for a solution is 10 per cent, made by gradually adding 10g of the dry material to 100ml of water at room temperature, or 100g to 1 litre, etc, keeping the ratio unchanged. Each 10ml of the solution will contain 1g of caustic soda. Be careful to prevent splashing when making the solution; rubber gloves and eye protection are sensible precautions.

Salt is used with direct and reactive dyes to promote an attraction between the dye and the fibre. With both dyes, it can be added dry to the dyebath but it may be difficult to measure small quantities, and in the case of reactive dyes, to dissolve it in a cold-water dyebath. It is more conveniently used as a 20 per cent solution made by dissolving 200g in 1 litre of boiling water. Each 5ml of this solution will contain 1g of salt.

Common salt (sodium chloride)

A dispersing agent is used with disperse dyes to keep their particles evenly distributed in the water of the dyebath. Without it they would tend to settle at the bottom of the bath. While it is possible to use a good quality detergent or soap solution for the purpose, better results are obtained from a proprietary compound specified by the dye manufacturer.

Dispersing agent

Dispersing agents are used in quite small amounts – typically 1 per cent of fibre weight; thus for 100g of fibre in a dyebath, 1ml of dispersing agent would be required. To avoid difficulties in measurement it is helpful to dilute the agent and then use proportionally more of the solution. A 10 per cent strength is suitable and can be made by mixing 100ml of dispersing agent in 1 litre of water.

Glauber's is used with acid levelling dyes as a restraining agent. By combining preferentially with the fibre at low dyebath temperatures it blocks dye take-up; as heat increases, the bond between it and the fibre is progressively weakened and it is slowly replaced by the dye molecules. This slow transfer of dye results in level dyeing.

Glauber's salt (sodium sulphate)

Glauber's is also used occasionally with direct dyes as an alternative to common salt, and with certain reactive dyes with which it produces a better performance.

Like common salt, Glauber's may be used dry but is more conveniently added to a dyebath in a liquid form. In the dry state it exists as crystals or as a calcined powder. 'Calcined' means that the substance has been heated until all moisture has been driven off. The powder is about 2¼ times stronger than the crystals and so less is used in making a stock solution.

The most convenient solution strength is 10 per cent, and it is made by dissolving 225g of the crystals, or 100g of the powder in 1 litre of boiling water. Each 10ml of the resulting solution contains 1g of the pure Glauber's salt.

Manutex is the trade name for a proprietary brand of sodium alginate, used to thicken dye solutions so that they can be applied by painting or block printing. Two grades are available: Manutex 'F' and 'RS'. The 'F' grade is coarser and makes a much thicker solution; the 'RS' grade is normally used for painting and printing solutions.

Manutex (sodium alginate)

To make up the thickener, soft water is required. This is provided by dissolving 1g (about a level teaspoonful) of a proprietary water softener (eg Calgon) in 15ml (about a dessertspoonful) of warm water at 40°C (105°F). Add a further 80ml (about 1fl oz) of cold water, stir, and then sprinkle 5g of Manutex over the surface. Stir continuously for 5–10 minutes until it is thoroughly smooth; it can be passed through a fine sieve to remove any remaining lumps. It is then ready to be added as required to a dye solution in the ratio 2 parts Manutex to 5 parts dye for printing, and 2 parts Manutex to 10 parts dye for painting.

Sodium dithionite or hydrosulphite

Sodium dithionite is used in vat dyeing to 'reduce' the dye; it absorbs oxygen dissolved in the water of the dyebath, leaving the hydrogen free to react with the dyestuff. It is also used as a stripping agent to assist in removing various cotton dyes from the fibre. It cannot be made into a solution as this would cause it to react with the water in which it was dissolved, thus losing its potency.

Urea

Urea is a compound of ammonia and carbon dioxide, and is used as a dissolving agent. Mixed with a reactive dye powder, it allows more to be dissolved in a given quantity of water than would otherwise be possible.

It is used as follows. Mix 10g (about $\frac{1}{3}$oz) of urea granules in 45ml (approximately $\frac{1}{2}$fl oz) of hot water at 70°C (160°F) and stir until it has dissolved. Add the required amount of dye powder – up to a maximum of 5g – and work it into the solution until all lumps have dissolved and the mixture has the smooth consistency of cream. Make up the volume to 100ml (approximately 1fl oz) with cold water. The solution is now ready for use.

Vinegar

See under Acids, p56.

Washing soda (sodium carbonate)

Soda is used with reactive dyes to promote the chemical reaction between the fibre and the dye molecules. It can be used dry, but like salt, it may be difficult to measure in small quantities and also to dissolve in a cold dyebath. It is usual to make it into a stock solution.

In the dry state soda is available as ordinary domestic crystals, or in its calcined form as 'soda ash'. The latter is about twice the strength of the former, and thus proportionally less is used in making a solution. A 10 per cent stock solution is convenient and is made by dissolving 200g of soda crystals, or 100g of soda ash, in 1 litre of boiling water. Each 10ml of this solution thus contains 1g of pure soda.

Wetting agent

A wetting agent is a type of detergent used in a separate bath to assist the penetration of dye into a fibre. It acts by reducing the surface tension of the water, thus allowing it to flow more readily into the cavities of a fibre to displace air and prepare the way for an effective take-up of dye.

Fastness ratings

Fastness is the ability of a dye to retain its colour and strength under all the conditions to which it will be exposed in use. Influences that can affect fastness are light, washing, heat, perspiration, atmospheric pollution, nature of the fibre, the dyeing process, and so on. For craft dyers, light and washing are the significant influences.

Light, and especially sunlight, can produce a reaction in a dye compound to partially decompose its structure and thus affect its colour. The visible change may be a simple loss of colour, but in some cases the colour itself can alter; both come within the term 'fading'. The ability of a dye to withstand fading – its lightfastness – can be measured by exposing a sample to daylight for an appropriate period and noting any changes that occur. In practice this can be a lengthy process, and in industry it is shortened by substituting an artificial light source for natural daylight. This is the Xenon lamp which has a closely controlled output that simulates daylight, and any colour changes it causes in dye samples are measured by comparison with standard shade cards, numbered from 1 to 8. Lightfastness tests are carried out on all industrial dyes to examine performance over a range of colour strengths; results are published by the dye manufacturers.

A rating of 1 indicates that the dye has a very poor lightfastness, while 8 – the maximum possible – says that it has an excellent resistance to fading. An acceptable performance depends to some extent upon the use of the dyed fibre. Garments, for example, that might possibly wear out before fading becomes significant could well be satisfied by a rating of, say, 4 or 5, but a rug or a wall hanging that would have little wear but a considerable exposure to light would merit a value of 6 or more in its dyes. The general rule is 'the higher the better' and manufacturer's information should be consulted if lightfastness is a concern.

Washing is a far more complicated matter because of the variety of detergents, soaps, processes, etc that can be used. Washfastness figures are obtained from a variety of tests designed to cover the range of laundering methods to which dyed fibres might be exposed, but for craftworkers it is sufficient to select from that range just the one that represents most closely domestic washing conditions.

This test looks for loss of colour from the sample during washing in a soap solution under specified conditions of temperature and duration, and examines any tendency of the dye to bleed to adjacent fibres. Results are

	Washfastness (out of 5)	Lightfastness (out of 8)
Wool dyes		
Acid milling	4	4–5
Acid levelling	4	4–5
Acid metal-complex	4–5	6–7
Reactive	5	6
Chrome	5	6
Cotton dyes		
Direct	3–4	6
Reactive	5	5–6
Vat	4–5	6–7
Azoic	4–5	6–7
Man-made fibres		
Disperse	5	6
These figures have been extracted from various manufacturers' literature and apply to dyes used at standard strength. If paler tints are dyed, fastness may be reduced.		

Fig 13
Comparative fastness ratings of various dyes

GENERAL DYEING INFORMATION

measured on a scale from 1 to 5, the lower figure indicating the worst performance.

As with lightfastness, the significance of a particular rating depends upon the use to be made of the dyed fibre. Items likely to undergo frequent washing require a rating of at least 3 and preferably 4 to be safe; if washing or cleaning will be less frequent – upholstery fabrics, for example – a lower value can be tolerated.

Different colours, even within the same type and brand of dye, can have different light and washfastness ratings because their chemical compositions are different. This should be borne in mind when selecting colours from a collection of dyes; do not rely upon them all having the same fastness ratings – choose each colour separately.

The table at Fig 13 shows the average light and washfastness ratings of the dyes reviewed in this book.

5
ACID DYES

The introduction of acid dyes in 1862 made compounds available that were soluble in water, had a natural affinity for wool and silk, and could be applied without a mordant. Their success led to further development into three main types: levelling, milling and metal-complex dyes. Each type is suitable for use in craftwork, and is described in this chapter together with suggested methods of use.

The word 'levelling' refers to the evenness with which dye is taken up by a fibre. Evenness is an important aspect of all dyeing, but essential when dyeing fabrics. Variations in the colour of raw fibre can be blended out when it is carded and spun into yarn: discrepancies in the colour of a yarn can be hidden when it is plied, or woven into a cloth, but errors in the dyeing of cloth remain obvious and cannot easily be corrected.

Levelling dyes

Levelling dyes were developed to avoid unevenness in fabric dyeing. Their molecules are small and light, and during the dyeing process they migrate from one part of the fibre to another before finally settling down in one place. This 'hunting for a home' results in an even distribution, and levelling dyes are sometimes called 'equalising' dyes because their molecules 'equalise' themselves over the fibre.

There is a penalty for this, however. Because the dye molecules have a capacity for movement on the fibre their attachment to it is necessarily weak; in consequence fastness to washing and finishing processes is only moderate. This is a general characteristic of levelling dyes, although some special varieties are made with improved fastness ratings.

The inherent evenness of these dyes is aided by the use of Glauber's salt in the dyebath to slow down the rate of attachment. At room temperatures the salt is taken up in preference to the dye, and thus blocks dye migration. As the dyebath is heated this situation reverses and the salt/fibre bond progressively weakens while the dye/fibre bond is stimulated; the greater binding forces of the dye then enable it to replace the salt.

Acid is also used to increase the positive charge on the fibre and thus promote the attachment of the negatively charged dye molecules. The weaker the bond between the fibre and the dye, the stronger the acid has to be. In industry sulphuric acid, or sometimes formic or phosphoric, is used to provide the strongly acidic conditions required (pH 2–3). For craft dyers acetic acid can be used instead, but will be needed in greater amounts to compensate for its comparative weakness.

Finally, the rate at which the dyebath is heated needs to be controlled.

Levelling dyes are worth considering by craftworkers when it is more important to obtain even colours than to have a high washfastness – although washfastness can be enhanced by soaping the fibre after dyeing.

61

The dyes are suitable for tapestries, embroideries, rugs and hangings, and in industry are used for carpets and dress fabrics, especially when mixtures of colours are required.

A typical procedure for using levelling dyes is as follows:

1 Make up the dyebath at 60°C (140°F) and to a liquor ratio of 50:1.

2 Add Glauber's salt at 10 per cent of the fibre weight. This equals 1ml of Glauber's solution per gram of fibre.

3 Add acetic acid in the form of vinegar. To compensate for its weakness compared with sulphuric acid, use 55 per cent of fibre weight. This is the equivalent of 0.5ml per gram of fibre.

4 Add the required amount of dye solution.

5 Stir the bath to mix all the ingredients thoroughly and then add the clean wetted fibre.

6 Heat the dyebath slowly and steadily to reach boiling point in 20 minutes. Note, however, that with silk the temperature should not rise above 80°C (175°F).

7 Simmer for 60 minutes.

8 Rinse the dyed fibre in warm water until it runs clear, and then transfer it to a soaping bath.

9 The soaping bath consists of water to a liquor ratio of 50:1, plus a little liquid soap or good quality detergent at the rate of 1ml per 2¼ litres.

10 Add the dyed fibre and bring the soaping bath to simmering point, 80°C (175°F), and treat it for 10 minutes at this temperature.

11 At the end of the period rinse the fibre in warm water, again until it runs clear, and then dry it away from direct heat and sunlight.

Milling dyes 'Milling' is the industrial process of fulling and finishing woollen cloth to achieve a specified shrinkage, density and size. It is demanding in terms of dye fastness and will wash out colours that are not securely bonded on the fibre, so milling dyes were developed to withstand this form of processing. They have larger, heavier molecules which do not move so readily in the dyebath as those of levelling dyes, but bond to the fibre very strongly and quickly, mostly at the point of first contact. This strong attachment results in very good washfastness, but their lack of mobility in the dyebath causes the molecules to cluster on the fibre, which leads to uneven colouring. This is a characteristic of milling dyes.

Some dye manufacturers recommend Glauber's salt as a restraining agent to counteract unevenness, while others suggest ammonium acetate or ammonium sulphate instead. The difference is related to the chemistry of the dyes themselves, and it is important to follow manufacturers' instructions. If Glauber's salt is used with a dye for which it is not recommended, it may act in the opposite manner to the one required and accelerate dye transfer instead of restraining it, leading to even greater unevenness.

Because milling dyes have a high affinity for protein fibres they do not require a strong acid in the dyebath. For ordinary types a pH of 5.5–6 is sufficient and is obtained by using acetic acid instead of sulphuric; a subclass of milling dyes known as 'super-milling' or 'neutral-dyeing' require even less acid (pH 5.5–7) and are used with ammonium sulphate.

The following procedure has been tested with milling dyes requiring ammonium sulphate as an assistant. Woollen yarn dyed to a reasonably even colour, is perfectly acceptable for knitting, crocheting, etc. On a significant area of single colour plain weaving, however, there were slight variations of tone, and for this type of project a levelling dye would be more suitable.

1 Make up the dyebath at 55–60°C (130–40°F) to a liquor ratio of 50:1.

2 Add ammonium sulphate at 4 per cent of the fibre weight; this is the equivalent of 0.4ml of 10 per cent solution per gram of fibre.

3 Add levelling agent at 2 per cent of fibre weight. This can be a suitable proprietary brand, or a few drops of a good quality detergent.

4 Stir the liquor to mix the ingredients and then add the clean wetted fibre.

5 Maintain the bath for 10 minutes at 55–60°C (130–40°F), moving the fibre from time to time to ensure an even exposure to the liquor.

6 After 10 minutes remove the fibre and add the required amount of dye. For standard strength colours use 2ml of stock solution per gram of fibre, down to 0.1ml for the palest tints and up to 4ml for the strongest hues. Stir the bath to mix in the dye and then replace the fibre.

7 Maintain the bath at the same temperature for a further 15 minutes, frequently moving the fibre, especially during the first 5 minutes or so.

8 After 15 minutes, slowly raise the temperature to reach boiling point in 40 minutes, gently turning the fibre from time to time during this period.

9 Once boiling point is reached, reduce the temperature to simmering, 95°C (205°F), to avoid felting, and continue at this level for about 15 minutes. Then remove the fibre and add 0.8ml of vinegar per gram.

10 Stir the bath and replace the fibre, and continue simmering for a further 20 minutes.

11 At the end of this period the fibre can be removed, cooled, rinsed and dried away from direct heat and out of direct sunlight.

An alternative type of dye for which Glauber's salt was specified would require a similar procedure except that at step 2 the salt and acetic acid would be used instead of ammonium sulphate. For example, Croda Colours recommendations for their type 3 acid dyes suggest 10 per cent of Glauber's salt and 1–3 per cent of acetic acid at 80 per cent strength at the initial setting of the bath. These amounts are the equivalent of 1ml of a 10 per cent Glauber's solution and 0.2–0.6ml of vinegar per gram of fibre. Step 9 would, of course, be omitted.

The colour circle on Plate 1 was dyed with neutral-dyeing milling dyes and shows a typical selection of the colours that can be obtained. The block of separate colours beneath were painted on paper using the same dyes at the same strength. The significance of these presentations is explained in Chapter 10, 'Choosing and Using Dyes'.

Metal-complex dyes

In their original form, introduced in 1915, metal-complex dyes required a strongly acidic dyebath (pH 2) and sulphuric acid was used at the rate of 8 per cent of the fibre weight. If the acidity was much less than this the colours tended to be uneven. Subsequently, various proprietary levelling agents were developed that allowed a weaker dyebath to be used, with benefit to the fibre. Dyes of this type are known as 1:1 metal-complex dyes, the ratio 1:1 indicating that the proportion of metal atoms to dye molecules is equal.

In 1949 a second form of the dyes appeared, called 1:2 dyes because of their different composition. These retained the high all-round fastness of the original type but had a higher affinity for protein fibre, and could be applied from a neutral or weakly acid dyebath (pH 6). These are the type mostly used today. Acetic acid or ammonium sulphate are used to provide the correct dyebath conditions, together with a levelling agent.

Metal-complex dyes produce muted colours, but extra brightness can be obtained by combining a metal-complex dye with a compatible super-milling dye. One drawback is the absence of a useful blue, which for reasons of pure chemistry cannot be made from a metal-complex dye compound. It is customary to use instead a compatible super-milling dye of appropriate hue.

Plate 4 shows a selection of fibres dyed with metal-complex dyes. The outer segment shows the dyes applied to woollen yarn; the next to nylon; then to mohair, a wool/acrylic/nylon blend, and finally to silk. All five fibres were dyed at standard strength, in the same dyebaths, and for the same time, so that directly comparable results could be obtained. Nylon can be seen to have taken the dye strongly with pure colours but some individuality in the black and browns; the wool/acrylic/nylon blend was spun from mixed staple fibre and the resulting yarn accepted colour to varying extents, giving a 'frosted' effect on a pastel background.

Other specimens on the plate are related to Chapter 11, 'Experimenting with Dyes', but were coloured with the same metal-complex dyes.

The procedure is this:

1 Make a dyebath at 50°C (120°F) to a liquor ratio of 50:1.

2 Add a recommended levelling agent at 0.3–1 per cent of the fibre weight. If it is difficult to measure small quantities of the levelling agent it can be diluted with a known amount of water, and proportionally more of the solution used.

3 Add ammonium sulphate at 3 per cent of the fibre weight. This is the equivalent of 0.3ml of a 10 per cent solution for each gram of fibre.

4 Stir the bath to mix all the ingredients and then add the clean wetted fibre, gently moving it to and fro to obtain an even exposure to the liquor.

5 Maintain the bath at 50°C (120°F) for 10 minutes, then remove the fibre and add the dye. Use 2ml of the stock solution per gram of fibre, down to 0.1ml for the palest tints, and up to 4ml for strong hues. Replace the fibre and move it in the liquor, especially during the first 5 minutes or so.

6 Heat the bath slowly to reach boiling point (except for silk) in 30 minutes. For silk, raise the temperature at the same rate but do not go above 80°C (175°F) or the lustre could be damaged.

7 When the required temperature is reached, stabilise the heat and continue dyeing just below a rolling boil, or at 80°C (175°F) for silk, for another 45 minutes, turning the fibre gently from time to time.

8 At the end of the dyeing period remove the fibre, allow it to cool and then rinse it in warm water. This is followed by a wash in a soap solution and a final rinse; it may then be dried away from direct heat and out of sunlight.

6
DIRECT DYES

The main disadvantage of direct dyes is their mediocre resistance to washing and water. Fig 13 on p59 shows that their washfastness is the lowest of all the dyes reviewed. For this reason they are best suited to applications where wet-fastness is not a prime consideration, eg furnishing fabrics, drapes and hangings.

However, it is possible to treat fibres after dyeing to improve washfastness, the process and substances varying with particular types of the dye. Most manufacturers make their own proprietary solutions that are applied from a second treatment bath; some of these chemicals can be hazardous and are best avoided in craftwork. An alternative of soaping was investigated for this book, and appears to be effective if one is prepared to accept a slight loss of colour strength. This could be compensated if necessary by increasing the strength of the dye to begin with and taking steps to improve dyebath exhaustion by adding more salt.

The experiments showed that two soaping treatments are advisable. After the first there is a significant loss of loose dye, but after the second the soaping bath remained virtually clear, indicating that no further significant loss had occurred. If washfastness is important, soaping appears to be a safe method of obtaining an acceptable performance. The process is included in the passage on dyeing procedure.

Lightfastness is not a problem. Direct dyes fall into two classes: those of ordinary grades having a good average performance, and special 'fast to light' grades having superior lightfastness. Reference to Fig 13 shows the latter can stand comparison to the best of all synthetic dyes.

Level-dyeing These dyes vary in their ability to produce even colouring; some are inherently level-dyeing while others are not. The Society of Dyers and Colourists has classified all the direct dyes in general use and placed them in three classes according to level-dyeing performance.

Class A dyes are all self-levelling and can be used without any special procedures; they comprise about 22 per cent of the type. Class B dyes need the addition of salt in increments to obtain even colours; about 57 per cent of direct dyes come in this group. Class C dyes require both salt and a controlled slow rise in dyebath temperature; the remaining 21 per cent of dyes belong in this group, including most of the blacks.

Experiments were carried out under craftroom conditions to assess each procedure, and no significant differences in performance were discovered. The process described later is the one that best meets the criteria of convenience and quality of colour.

Salt is used with direct dyes to promote dye transfer and assist dyebath exhaustion. Both common and Glauber's salt are suitable; one authority claims that Glauber's salt is preferable for pastel colours, but we have no proof of this. Salt can be added in liquid form as a solution, or in its dry state; if Glauber's salt is being used dry, the amounts should be doubled.

Dyebath quantities

Dyebath exhaustion can be improved by reducing the amount of water, thus increasing the concentration of dye. Under these circumstances less salt is required. For even colouring it is better to minimise the amount of water, making sure the fibre is covered, and correspondingly reduce the quantity of salt; very pale tints can be dyed without any salt at all.

Fig 14 shows the average amounts of salt required for various liquor ratios – the figures have been derived from dye manufacturers' recommendations.

Liquor ratio	Salt, *per gram of fibre*	
	Dry (g)	20% soln (ml)
10:1	0.05	0.25
20:1	0.10	0.50
30:1	0.15	0.75
40:1	0.20	1.00
50:1	0.25	1.25
60:1	0.30	1.50

Fig 14 *Salt requirements per gram of fibre at various liquor ratios*

Direct dyes produce robust colours on fibres and yarns – blues especially tend to be strong and need to be used with caution in mixtures with other colours, or they may saturate the blend. Plate 2 shows direct dyes at the bottom three rows; with the exception of black, all the colours were dyed at 1 per cent, 0.5 per cent and 0.1 per cent strengths. Black was dyed according to the maker's instructions at 3 per cent, 1.5 per cent, and 0.3 per cent. The green and violet respectively were mixed from 1½ parts of yellow plus ½ part of blue, and from 1⅔ parts of red plus ⅓ part of blue. Note how in each case the blue tends to predominate over the other colour.

Direct dyes are made into stock solutions just like other dyes, but the method is slightly different. The powder is pasted with a little cold water and worked to a smooth consistency, and finally dissolved in boiling water, all as before, but at this point the solution is brought back to the boil for a few minutes and then filtered through a fine mesh sieve or a fine filter cloth (old tights are excellent) before being cooled, made up to the full amount, and bottled.

The dyeing process

Salt can be used dry or as a 20 per cent solution. If it is used dry the dyebath must be stirred until it has completely dissolved before adding any other ingredients.

1 Add water to the dyepot in the chosen liquor ratio. Check that there is enough to cover the fibre.

2 Add the salt; the amount required can be determined from Fig 14.

3 Add the required amount of dye solution. Plate 2 can be used as a guide to the strength of colour resulting from various amounts. Stir the bath thoroughly to mix the contents.

4 Now enter the clean wetted fibre, moving it to and fro in the bath to obtain an even exposure to the dye liquor. This movement is especially important during the first 2–3 minutes to ensure level colouring.

5 Bring the dyebath to a boil as rapidly as possible, moving the fibre fairly often to maintain an even exposure to the dye.

6 Maintain boiling temperature for a further 45 minutes, then remove the dyebath from the heat and allow the fibres to cool naturally in the dye liquor until they can be handled comfortably; this will be at a temperature of roughly 30–40°C (85–105°F). They can then be rinsed in warm water.

7 It is important to watch the level of the dyebath during the boiling period in case evaporation losses reduce the amount of liquor to a point where it no longer covers the fibre. If a significant loss has occurred, the liquid should be topped up with boiling water.

8 Soaping is not normally undertaken with direct dyes but is beneficial in removing loose dye during hand-dyeing procedures. Losses during subsequent washing are thus reduced and wet-fastness is improved. The procedure is described in Chapter 4 and should be followed twice in succession.

9 After soaping, the fibre should be rinsed in warm water until it runs clear, and then dried away from direct heat and strong sunlight.

7
REACTIVE DYES

These are the dyes that react chemically with a fibre to form a bond that is stronger and more permanent than a conventional physical attachment. They were originally named 'cellulose reactive' because they were developed for use on cellulose materials like cotton, linen, and the reconstituted fibre, viscose rayon; today they are usually called 'fibre reactive' or just 'reactive' since the family has grown to include types for colouring protein fibres as well as cellulose.

Reactive dyes produce their most brilliant colours on mercerised cotton, but wool and silk can also be dyed. Silk takes the dye very well, but sometimes with alterations in hue.

Dyeing is carried out either cold or hot according to the type of dye being used. An alkaline dyebath is necessary to allow the chemical reaction to take place and is provided by adding sodium carbonate in the form of ordinary washing soda crystals or as soda ash (which is the dry powdered form of the chemical and about twice as strong). Common salt, sodium chloride, is used to promote an attraction between the cellulose fibres and the molecules of dye to enhance the transfer of colour from the dyebath.

Cold-water dyes of the 'domestic' type, sold under such brand names as 'Punch', 'Ideal' and 'Dylon', are basically cold-water reactives. In some cases a proprietary fixative is used instead of soda, but common salt is normally required as usual. The main difference between these dyes and the conventional reactives is in their colour blending. Conventional dyes are made in basic colours such as red, blue, yellow, green, and so on, which can be mixed in varying proportions to produce thousands of different colours. The household reactives are marketed in a range of pre-blended fashion colours; these can be used together but lack the flexibility in colour mixing of the simple hues. It is also difficult to establish the strength of these dyes and thus to control the depth of colour that will be produced.

This information is additional to the general advice given in Chapter 1. **Safety**

There are special safety considerations applying to reactive dyes. Because of their nature the powders of both hot- and cold-water varieties can cause sensitivities to develop in some (but only some) people if the powders are inhaled. Thereafter those persons are likely to suffer a reaction whenever they are exposed – wheezy cough, occasional blocked nose, etc, roughly similar to hay fever. Naturally, the degree of hazard is related to the scale of exposure, and is greatest in the chemical and dyeing industries where large amounts of the materials are handled. Craftworkers are unlikely to use more than a tiny fraction of those quantities, and their degree of risk is correspondingly very much lower; nevertheless, they should be careful to avoid creating or inhaling dust from these dye powders. The cold-water variety have a greater potential for causing harm because they are the most reactive.

Dye manufacturers responded to the problem by treating the powders to suppress dust by making the dyes in the alternative forms of granules – which are inherently less dusty – and where possible as liquids – which of course, produce no dust at all. In parallel with this, industrial dyehouses are equipped with extraction plants to eliminate any hazard to employees.

Craftworkers should use a simple dustmask when handling reactive dye powders in the dry state, and be careful that their methods do not create dust. Individuals known to suffer from asthma or other bronchial ailments would be wise to avoid using reactive dyes in powder form; liquid or granular preparations are to be preferred. Alternatively, direct dyes of the 'fast to light' grade might be used instead, especially if the dyed fibre was not to be exposed to frequent washing, or if high washfastness was not important.

Cold-water reactive dyes

Cold-water dyes progressively lose strength once they get wet. This loss may not be significant in craftwork unless an exactly matching colour is required: good colour strengths are obtainable even several months after mixing. In industry, however, where precise hues are required, any reduction in colour is unacceptable and the life of mixed dye is limited to two or three days. The loss of colour strength can be slowed down by storage in a refrigerator after mixing; in these conditions the two- or three-day life may be extended to two or three weeks before significant change occurs.

Despite the care needed when using them, cold-water reactives have a number of advantages for craftworkers:

- The dyebath is used cold, so heatproof equipment is unnecessary and metal dyepans may be replaced by plastic bowls, empty margarine containers or even clean yoghurt pots.
- Heaters and stoves are not required so dyeing can be undertaken virtually anywhere.
- Dye solutions can be thickened and applied by brush like paints, or used for block or silk-screen printing, or through a spray-gun.
- The dyes are ideal for batik and general resist processes where heat would melt wax or damage gutta preparations.

Their disadvantages are:

- A limited life if full-strength colours are required. In colour-sensitive applications they should be mixed just before use.
- A low-penetrating power into the fibre. This makes them more suitable for softly twisted yarns and loose fibres than tightly woven or twisted material.
- A reduction and ultimate loss of reactivity and hence dyeing fastness, if they are heated above the recommended temperatures. This feature can be an asset, however, if one wishes to stop the dyeing reaction once a certain point in a process has been reached, eg in some painting and printing operations.

There are two methods available: the incremental process used in industry in which salt and soda are introduced in one or more increments at specified times during the dyeing cycle, and a simplified method in which all the ingredients are placed in the dyebath at the same time at the beginning of the procedure.

Dyeing procedure for cotton, linen, etc

Experiments with both methods under craftroom conditions showed that the all-in-one system is quite suitable for craft dyers and gives results that are marginally but consistently better. This is the process now described: it is assumed that stock solutions of salt and soda will have been made up, and the fibres prepared, as suggested in Chapter 4. Remember, however, that if the maximum depth of colour is wanted, the dye solution should be mixed just before it is required for use.

1 The liquor ratio of the dyebath depends to some extent upon the shape of the dyepot and the bulk of the fibres. In a conventional dyepot a ratio of 30:1 may be a good average value, but in a narrow, upright vessel the ratio might be reduced to, say, 10:1. The guideline is to use as little liquid as possible but to ensure that the fibres are at all times adequately covered. The dyebath should be lukewarm at a temperature of 30°C (85°F) maximum.

2 Stir in the required amount of dye solution. For pale tints use 0.5ml/g, or even less for very pale colours. Note, however, that the less dye there is in the bath, the more thinly it will colour the fibre and the more obvious will be any variations in evenness. Particular care is needed when dyeing very pale colours, and to help avoid unevenness the amount of salt can be halved, or even none at all used. Such adjustments reduce the attraction between the dye and the fibre and thus slow down the rate of dye transfer; the addition of a few drops of a good quality detergent or hair shampoo may also be helpful in acting as a levelling agent. Average strength colours are obtained from 3 to 4ml/g of dye solution, and strong hues from 5ml/g up to, say, 6ml/g. Above this amount the fibre is unlikely to absorb any more dye.

3 Next, add the salt solution. As with the dye, the amount required varies according to the depth of colour (dye strength) being used. Fig 15 gives the amount of 20 per cent salt solution, in ml/g, to be used for various dye strengths. Some dyes – turquoise and some blues, for example – are better used with Glauber's salt than common salt. Always check manufacturer's or supplier's information in case there are special requirements.

4 Now add the soda solution. The amount varies with dye strength. Fig 16 gives the amount of 10 per cent soda solution required at various dye strengths.

5 Stir the dyebath thoroughly to mix the ingredients and then add the clean wetted fibre, moving it gently to and fro to ensure an even exposure to the dye liquor. This is especially important during the first 5 minutes, and particularly with pale tints, to obtain even colouring.

6 Continue dyeing for 120 minutes at the original temperature of 30°C (85°F), gently stirring the fibre every 10–15 minutes or so. For some dyes it may be

Fig 15 *Salt requirements for cold-water reactive dyes*

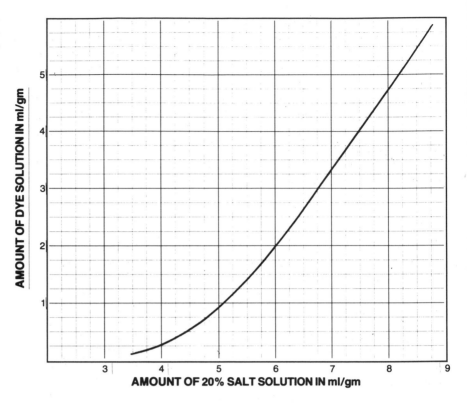

Fig 16 *Soda requirements for cold-water reactive dyes*

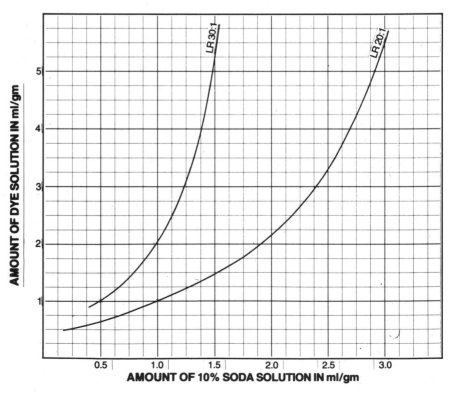

necessary to increase the temperature during this time – Turquoise MX-G, for example, which requires 60°C (140°F) for the last 20 minutes of dyeing. Information on such requirements is published by dye manufacturers.

7 When dyeing is complete the fibre should be rinsed in warm running water until it runs clear. (A considerable loss of colour is likely to occur – as much as 20–30 per cent – as unreacted dye is washed away. This is normal.) When the water runs clear transfer the fibre to a soaping bath for further treatment (see Chapter 4, 'Soaping').

8 After soaping, the fibre should be dried away from direct heat and sunlight. Hanked yarn may benefit from a little light tension while drying.

Wool can be dyed with cold-water reactive dyes, but the normal process has to be changed. Salt and soda are not required because wool is a protein fibre, not cellulose, and needs an acid dyebath. Acetic acid is used instead and the dyebath is heated, so the process becomes very similar to normal acid dyeing on wool. It is sometimes difficult to obtain even colours by this method, especially if there are variations in the quality of the wool, and hues are likely to be paler and weaker than those obtained from acid dyes. There is perhaps not a great deal to commend the procedure, but as it may be the only means of getting colour on wool if other dyes are not immediately available, the process is briefly described.

Dyeing procedure for wool

1 Make a dyebath to a liquor ratio of approximately 30:1; more water may be needed for fleece. No heat is required at this stage and the bath should be at room temperature, say, 15°C (60°F).

2 Add ordinary vinegar at the rate of 0.3ml/g.

3 Add the dye. As an average, use 1–2ml/g for pale tints, and 4–5ml/g for standard strength colours.

4 Stir the dyebath to mix the contents and then add the clean wetted fibres, moving them gently in the liquor to obtain an even exposure to the dye.

5 Heat the bath slowly to reach 50°C (120°F) in about 30–35 minutes. Steady, slow heating is important for even dyeing: it is better to heat too slowly than too fast. A low temperature can readily be corrected but one that is too high may already have caused damage that cannot be undone by reducing the temperature of the bath.

6 Continue dyeing at 50°C (120°F) for 30 minutes, then raise the temperature to boiling for 5 minutes to fix the dye.

7 The fibres are now cooled slowly to prevent shrinking. The bath and its contents can be removed from heat and allowed to cool naturally, or the fibres can be lifted out very carefully to cool in free air. When cool enough to handle they should be rinsed in warm water and then washed gently in warm soapy water; this is followed by a final rinse, after which they may be dried away from direct heat and out of direct sunlight. Hanks of wool might benefit from a little light tension while drying.

Dyeing procedure for silk Silk can be coloured successfully with cold-water reactive dyes, even though it is a protein fibre. It takes the dye very readily and to avoid uneven colours it is usually necessary to use a levelling agent to retard dye transfer, rather than an assistant to stimulate it. Some colours – black, for example – may show a change in hue and it is advisable to experiment and compile a sample card to know just what to expect from this dye/fibre combination. There are two processes, one requiring formic acid and the other just soda and Glauber's salt; the latter is preferred because it produces more even colouring, and also uses salt and soda solutions already prepared for other dyestuffs.

The use of soda – an alkali – with a protein fibre, may be questioned. Silk is four times more alkali-resistant than wool or hair fibres, and it suffers no harm from exposure to soda provided the quantity is not excessive and all residues are rinsed out at the end of the process.

Silk fibre should be degummed before dyeing to prevent the formation of a dye/gum combination that will leave the silk hard and dull, and be difficult to remove (see Chapter 4, 'Fibre Preparation and Finishing').

The preferred method of dyeing silk is this:

1 Make the dyebath to a 30:1 liquor ratio and at room temperature, say 15°C (60°F).

2 Add Glauber's salt solution at the rate of 7.5ml/g (see Chapter 4, 'Dyebath Assistants').

3 Add the appropriate amount of dye solution. For pale tints use 1–2ml/g, and for medium colours 2–3ml/g. Stir the bath to mix the contents.

4 Add the silk and begin dyeing at room temperature. Move the fibre gently in the liquor, especially during the first 5 minutes, to obtain an even exposure to the dye liquor. After 20 minutes slowly raise the temperature to reach 50°C (120°F) in about 30 minutes, and then continue to dye at this level for another 15 minutes.

5 At the end of this 15-minute period remove the silk and add soda to the bath at the rate of 0.6ml/g. Stir well and then replace the silk and continue dyeing for a final period of 40 minutes at the same temperature of 50°C (120°F).

6 The silk must now be rinsed in cold water and transferred to a soaping bath. This bath is not quite the same as that described in Chapter 4. It should contain enough water to cover the fibre, plus a little liquid soap but *not* detergent, which is too harsh for silk. Add soda solution at rate of 0.3ml/g.

7 Heat this bath to 85°C (185°F) and treat the silk at this temperature for 10 minutes, followed by two cold rinses. The first rinse should contain a tablespoonful of ordinary vinegar to neutralise any soda remaining in the fibre, and to improve its lustre and feel. The second rinse is pure water to remove the vinegar. The silk can now be dried away from direct heat and out of direct sunlight.

Hot-water reactive dyes are a logical development of the cold-water types. However, they are less reactive and have a longer life after being mixed with water, and can remain in solution for up to four weeks or more without noticeably losing strength. To compensate for their lower reactivity they need more salt and soda in the dyebath, and a higher dyebath temperature – hence their name. The higher dyeing temperature results in improved penetration of the dye into the fibre, and this makes hot-water reactives particularly suitable for dyeing highly twisted yarn or closely woven cloth. Their colours are just as brilliant as the cold-water types and their fastness characteristics are similar.

Hot-water reactive dyes

Hot-water reactives are made as powders, grains and liquids to overcome the problems of dust inhalation, and in the case of liquids to simplify mixing procedures as well. The liquid forms may not always be as strong as the powders and grains, and care should be taken when using them to be sure that the correct amounts are measured for use. Manufacturer's literature should always be consulted on this point.

In industry hot-water reactive dyes can be applied by three processes: incremental, semi-incremental, and all-in-one – the choice between them depending upon the type of dyeing machinery being used, and to a lesser extent upon the particular colour being dyed. All three methods were tested under craftroom conditions; as the samples dyed by the all-in-one method produced the best results it is the process recommended for use with this type of reactive dye.

Dyeing procedure for cotton, linen, etc

1 Make the dyebath to a 30:1 liquor ratio and at room temperature – 15°C (60°F).

2 Add the dye. For pale tints use 0.5–1ml/g; average colours need 2–3ml/g and strong tones require 4ml/g or more.

3 Add salt solution in an amount appropriate to the strength of colour being dyed. Fig 17 indicates the amounts to be used for various dye strengths. Note that mercerised cotton and viscose rayon require less salt than un-mercerised fibres.

4 Add soda solution in a quantity related to dye strength as shown in Fig 18.

5 Stir the bath thoroughly to mix the solutions and then add the clean and wetted fibre, moving it gently to and fro, especially during the first 5–10 minutes, to ensure an even exposure to the dye liquor.

6 Leave the bath at room temperature for 15 minutes to allow the fibre to absorb and react to the solutions. At the end of this period raise the temperature slowly to reach 80°C (175°F) in about 30 minutes, still moving the fibre occasionally.

7 Once working temperature has been reached, continue dyeing for 60 minutes. The fibre should then be removed and rinsed in warm running

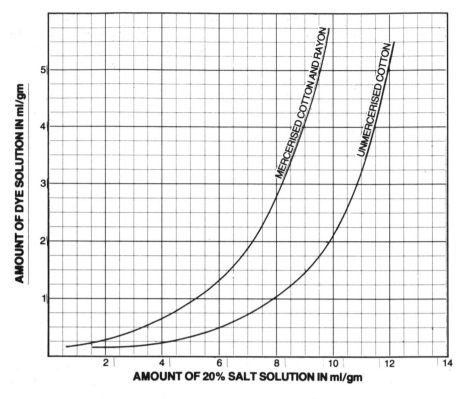

Fig 17 *Salt requirements for hot-water reactive dyes*

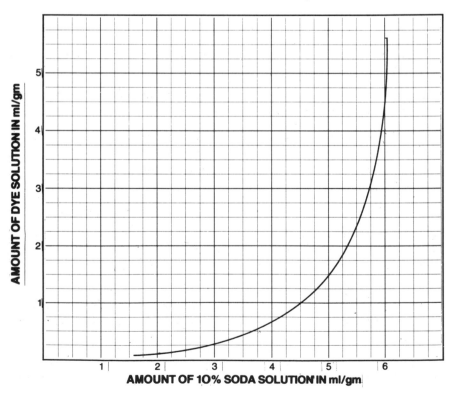

Fig 18 *Soda requirements for hot-water reactive dyes*

water until it runs clear, followed by treatment in a soaping bath (see Chapter 4, 'Soaping').

8 When soaping is complete, the fibre should be rinsed again, and then dried away from direct heat and sunlight.

Hot-water reactive dyes will colour wool in the same way as cold-water dyes, but, with the exception of one or two colours, only pastel hues are likely to result. Better colours can be obtained by using the special reactive dyes introduced in the early 1960s specifically for use on wool. These create an exceptionally good fibre/dye bond, resulting in excellent wash- and lightfastness.

Dyeing procedure for wool

Dyeing time varies with the depth of colour, strong hues requiring up to as much as three times longer than pale tints. A compatible levelling agent is necessary to promote even colouring and dyebath exhaustion.

Silk can be coloured with hot-water reactive dyes in exactly the same way as with cold-water dyes, except that the dyeing temperature at stage 4 of the cold-water process is increased to 70°C (160°F). Quantities, times and after-treatments all remain the same.

Dyeing procedure for silk

Reactive dyes of both cold- and hot-water types are extremely useful: their versatility, brilliant hues and ease of application make them very suitable for craftwork.

Conclusion

The upper half of Plate 2 shows cold-water dyes applied to mercerised cotton yarn at 0.1, 0.5, 1, 2 and 3ml/g strengths. The middle row of the three presents the dyes as basic colours; the top row shows the effect of mixing six of them with an equal amount of yellow to illustrate blending, while the third row shows them muted by being mixed with a half quantity of black. Note the effect of contrast of tone at the interfaces between the various dye strengths, particularly the blue and red specimens.

Examples of cold-water dyes applied by spraying are shown by the three small hanks in Plate 9. The dyes were used at different strengths and by different methods, all described in Chapter 11, 'Spray-dyeing'.

8

VAT DYES

Indigo was the first of the vat dyes, and was so called because at one time the process of using it involved old wine vats. It does not dissolve in water and cannot be used to colour fibre by the traditional methods of heating in a dyebath – its chemical form has to be changed before its colour can be released.

This transformation is brought about by a process called 'reduction', in which oxygen is removed from a dyebath containing indigo, leaving the hydrogen ion free to act on the dye. The dye is then transformed into its colourless 'leuco' form, named from the Greek *leukos*, meaning white. If the dyebath is sufficiently alkaline this leuco dye will dissolve, and can then transfer to a fibre.

Before modern technology evolved, indigo was reduced by fermentation in water or stale urine (male, and to be collected first thing in the morning) together with bran, bread, fruit and, at one time, woad as well, which was used as a 'starter'. It was these mixtures that were reacted in the wine vats – which was perhaps logical since fermentation was what they were made for. However, the process was unsavoury, time-consuming, and depended to a considerable extent upon the skill of the dyers in getting the mixture and conditions just right. It was quite unsuited to the needs of the embryo synthetic dye industry.

The chemical reagent sodium dithionite, or hydrosulphite as it is alternatively known, had been recognised as another way of reducing the dye, but initially it was too expensive for commercial use. After some years of research and experiment a way was found of making it more cheaply. At the same time efforts were being made to synthesise indigo so that a dye of greater strength, consistent quality and ready availability could be supplied to the industrial dyehouses. It was the knowledge gained from these two developments that prepared the way for the production of other, similar dyes – blues and yellows in 1901, orange and purple in 1904, and so on. These were all based on the chemistry of indigo, and because of their similarity to their parent they were also known as vat dyes.

In the course of time two varieties of vat dye emerged. One is based on indigo and known as the 'indigoid' type; the other was developed from anthracine – a coal-tar product – and is called the 'anthraquinoid' group. Both have to be reduced to their leuco form and applied from a neutral or slightly alkaline dyebath, and after dyeing both have to be reoxidised for their true colour to develop on a fibre. The indigoid types require less caustic in the dyebath and are thus kinder to fibres that are alkali-sensitive, but they are not quite as fast as the anthraquinoid group. These are best for cotton and linen because their excellent washfastness stands up to the severe laundering frequently experienced by cotton goods, while the higher alkalinity in their dyebaths can be withstood by those fibres. They are used when the highest dye performance is required, and by reference to Figure 13 their all-round fastness can be seen to equal the best of all the dyes reviewed.

Vat dyes are available in granular, liquid and powder forms. The liquids and grains are easiest to use as they disperse immediately into a dyebath, but note that some of the liquid preparations may be weaker than the corresponding grains or powders, and quantities may need adjustment. Powdered dyes have to be pasted before they will disperse; the method is described in Chapter 4, 'Dye Solutions', except that alcohol is used instead of water – methylated spirits are quite suitable.

The amount of caustic soda required depends to some extent upon the colour of a dye – in reality, its chemical composition, but this is correlated to its colour. The yellows, oranges and browns require more than the reds, blues, violets and greens, although there are exceptions. Dyes are classed as 'Method 1' if they require the larger amount, and as 'Method 2' if they need less, and these distinctions are shown in dye manufacturers' pattern cards. The dyeing procedure presented later quotes the caustic requirements for both types.

Fibres have to be well wetted (see Chapter 4, 'Fibre Preparation'), and they must never be allowed to rise above the surface of a dyebath or premature oxidation of the exposed parts will occur; this may cause uneven colouring and possibly reduced rub-fastness.

Dyeing procedure

Modern vat dyes exist in various forms adapted to meet differing conditions, and they can be applied to fibre by a variety of methods. Three of these could be of interest to craft dyers.

The 'vatting' process

In this process the dye is first made into a solution or stock 'vat' – the present-day counterpart of the old indigo vat. A quantity of dye is dissolved in a measured amount of water to which appropriate quantities of caustic soda and sodium dithionite are added. The dye reduces in this solution, and amounts of it are then used in a dyebath in proportion to the weight of fibre to be coloured. Dyeing can take place at 50–60°C (120–140°F) if 'warm-dyeing' vat dyes are used, or at 25–30°C (75–85°F) with the 'cold-dyeing' variety. The latter are somewhat less effective and to improve their performance common salt is also used in the dyebath.

The 'semi-pigmentation' process

Dye is dispersed (not dissolved) in a cold dyebath; fibre is then added and worked in the dispersion for about 10 minutes. During this time the particles of dye distribute themselves evenly over the fibre, ultimately to assist in level colouring. At the end of the 10-minute period appropriate quantities of caustic soda and sodium dithionite are added and the reduction of the dye takes place on the fibre. This is then worked for a further period, after which the dyebath is slowly heated to operating temperature, 50–60°C (120–140°F), and dyeing carried out for 30–40 minutes. This process is suited to soft fibres as the dyes do not have very great powers of penetration. It is simple to follow as all the ingredients are added at substantially the same time.

The 'pre-pigmentation' process This is useful for fabrics, or cops or cones of yarn that require greater dye penetration. A suitable dye is dispersed in the dyebath and the fibre added. The unreacted dye is then induced to attach itself to the fibre by the gradual addition of salt. Common salt may be used, or caustic soda (sodium hydroxide), depending upon the nature of the fibre. The dyebath is slowly heated to 50–60°C (120–140°F), and dyeing carried out for approximately 35–40 minutes.

Irrespective of which method is used, dyed fibres have to be aired to allow reoxidation of the dye to occur, and its true colour to develop. In craftwork this can be achieved by simple airing, but in industry where the time required is unacceptable, chemical oxidation is used. The dyed fibres are treated in a bath containing hydrogen peroxide with a little sodium bicarbonate sometimes added to neutralise any remaining caustic.

Of the three methods outlined, the second – semi-pigmentation – is the one preferred by the authors, and is the basis of the procedure now described.

Method **1** Make a dyebath with soft water at 20°C (70°F) and to a nominal 30:1 liquor ratio, but bear in mind that the fibre must remain submerged and use more water if necessary.

2 Add the dye. For standard strength colours use 3 per cent of the fibre weight, ie 0.03g/g, but for black use 10 per cent, ie 0.10g/g. Stir the bath to produce an even dispersion.

3 Wearing rubber gloves, add the wetted fibre and work it in the liquor for approximately 10 minutes.

4 Remove the fibre and add caustic soda solution (see Chapter 4, 'Dyebath Assistants') at a rate of 1.5ml/g (Method 1 dyes), or 0.8ml/g (Method 2 dyes). Replace the fibre and stir the bath.

5 Sprinkle sodium dithionite over the surface of the bath at a rate of 0.2g for each gram of fibre. Allow it to settle in the liquid and then very gently work the fibre for 10 minutes, taking care not to cause splashes or bubbles which could introduce air into the bath.

6 At the end of this period, *slowly* increase the temperature of the dyebath to reach 60°C (140°F) in about 30 minutes.

7 Dye at 60°C (140°F) for 30 minutes.

8 When dyeing is complete, remove the fibre, squeeze out drips but do not rinse, and hang in the air to oxidise. Leave it for at least 30 minutes and preferably for as long as possible – even overnight.

9 Finally, rinse the fibre and treat it in a soaping bath (see Chapter 4, 'Soaping'). This is important to remove any loose dye and to assist the development of true fastness and colour. After soaping, the fibre should be given a final rinse, and then dried away from direct heat.

9
DISPERSE DYES

As their name suggests, these dyes are dispersions of particles in water; they do not dissolve into a solution. If they are left undisturbed the particles tend to sink to the bottom of the dyebath. This is obviously unacceptable when dyeing, so a chemical called a 'dispersing agent' is added to the bath to keep the dye evenly distributed in the water.

Disperse dyes can be used to colour acetate, acrylic, nylon and polyester fibres, and mixtures of them, but different colour strengths will be developed on each. There are some variations in procedure for each fibre, so in the passages that follow a general process will be described first and be followed by notes on the variations, under the fibre headings.

1 A dyebath is made to a wide liquor ratio of 50:1. This is because man-made fibres tend to have a more open and bulky texture than wool or cotton, and need more water to ensure immersion. The temperature of the bath should be about 50°C (120°F) and it should have a pH of 5–5.5.

General dyeing procedure

2 The dispersing agent is added next (see Chapter 4, 'Dyebath Assistants'). The amount required is determined by the weight of fibre being coloured; Fig 19 gives the quantities recommended for various fibre weights.

3 Add the dye to the bath, shaking the bottle thoroughly to dislodge any sediment and bring it back into suspension before measuring out the amount required. For standard strength colours use 2ml/g of the dye liquid, decreasing to 0.1ml/g for very pale tints, or increasing to 4ml/g or more for rich tones – especially blacks.

4 Next add the clean wetted fibre, moving it gently to and fro in the bath to ensure an even exposure to the dye.

5 Heat the bath very slowly to reach boiling point in about 30 minutes, then reduce the temperature to simmering or slightly less to prevent any fibre damage due to a rolling boil.

6 Dye at 90–95°C (195–205°F) for 30–40 minutes, moving the fibre as little as possible, and then only very gently.

7 When dyeing is complete the fibre should be treated as described in the appropriate section. Once it is cool enough to handle it should be transferred to a soaping bath. This is not quite the same as the bath described in Chapter 4. It should contain enough water to cover the fibre, plus a small amount of soap solution – Fig 20 gives the quantities required for various fibre weights. Heat the bath to 50°C (120°F) and treat the fibre at this temperature for about 15 minutes. It may then be cooled, rinsed and dried.

Fig 19 *Dispersing agent required for various fibre weights*

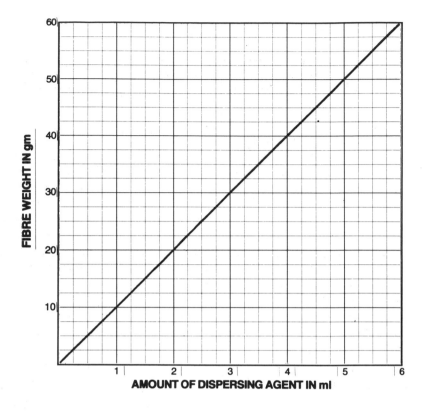

Fig 20 *Soap solution required for various fibre weights*

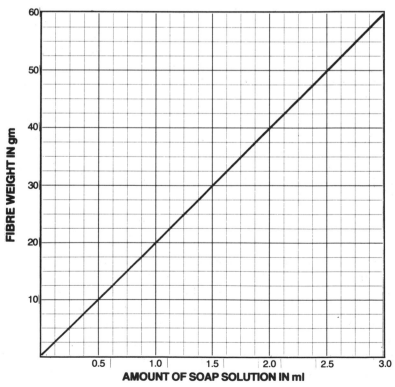

Acetate fibres may be encountered on their own but more often in blends with other fibres, eg acetate/wool. They can be coloured quite readily by the general process.

Dyeing particular fibres/*Acetate*

Acrylic fibres are easy to dye and they take a good colour, but are vulnerable to physical damage when hot and are readily distorted by careless treatment. For this reason it is advisable to keep the temperature of the dyebath below 85°C (185°F) at stages 5 and 6 of the general procedure. After dyeing, acrylic fibre should not be removed from the bath as described at stage 7, but left to cool in the dye liquor to 60°C (140°F) or less. It is then rinsed and soaped as described.

Acrylic

Polyester fibre is not widely encountered on its own, appearing more often in blended yarns for weaving or knitting. It is not as easy to dye as other man-made fibres because it has a very tight molecular structure that makes dye penetration difficult. This causes it to absorb dye very slowly and it needs extended dyeing periods to develop colours significantly stronger than pastel tints.

Polyester

There are two ways of speeding up the process: dyeing at an elevated temperature, and dyeing with the aid of a carrier.

Elevated temperatures (above 100°C (210°F)) can be obtained if dyeing is carried out under pressure. This entails the use of special equipment, but under these conditions temperatures from 125°C to 130°C (255°F to 265°F) can be reached and dyeing times dramatically reduced. The process is similar to dyeing in a domestic pressure cooker, and for craft use a pressure cooker can be used if care is taken not to overload it and block the safety valve. It should be set to operate at its maximum pressure which is usually about 15 psi; at this level a temperature of 120°C (250°F) is likely to be reached. The difference between a pressure cooker and industrial equipment is really one of size. Not much more than 25–30g (approx 1oz) of fibre can be dyed safely in a pressure cooker, whereas pressurised dyeing machinery is designed to accommodate much larger amounts at a time.

Dyeing time can also be reduced by adding an auxiliary chemical called a carrier to the dyebath. This has the effect of separating the molecules of the fibre, thus allowing dye penetration, and is introduced at stage 2 of the general process, after the dispersing agent. The amount required depends upon the dye manufacturer's advice, but typically could be 0.5 per cent of fibre weight. Such small amounts are difficult to measure accurately and it is more convenient to dilute the compound into a 5 per cent solution, and then to use 20 times as much.

After dyeing, polyester fibre is treated as described at stage 7 of the general process.

Blends of different fibres take disperse dyes according to their main constituent. Some, such as nylon/acrylic, show a greater richness and strength of colour than others like wool/acrylic. Plate 3 shows a range of ordinary blended yarns dyed in seven colours using Sandoz 'Artisil' dyes according to the general process. With one exception all the fibres were

Fibre blends

white – the exception being a grey yarn, included to show how colours can be muted by being dyed on a grey fibre as an alternative to using 'greyed' dyes on a white fibre.

The samples shown on Plate 3 and the results obtained with them are as follows, starting at the top and reading clockwise.

100% Wool   This fibre was used as a 'control' to provide a comparison against which to assess the other blends. It does not dye in the true sense, instead being just 'surface stained'. Tones are slightly muted and rub-fastness and washfastness are usually low. There is some slight distortion of colours: yellows acquire an ochre bias, blues show a colour shift towards turquoise, and black takes a reddish-brown tinge.

50% acrylic/
40% nylon/
10% wool   These three fibres had been blended in staple form and then spun into a composite yarn. Each individual fibre took colour slightly differently; the acrylic strands showed up palely against the stronger colours of the nylon component to create an impression of 'frosting' at close range, but at a distance the colours were bright and even.

60% wool/
40% acrylic   This combination produced very pure colours but somewhat less intense than those from some other mixtures. The yarn retained a very good lustre and would be well suited to dyeing pastel tints.

55% nylon/
45% acrylic   Disperse dyes produced their richest colours on this yarn, especially in yellow and black. The dyeing was even with good penetration. The fibres had been blended in staple form and then spun into a composite yarn, as with the acrylic/nylon/wool blend previously described. A similar 'frosted' effect resulted especially on the heavier colours – blue, red, black, violet and orange.

Plate 5 *Yarn stripping, showing proprietary stripping agent on various hanks.* (Left) *Cotton hanks dyed with reactive dyes.* (Right) *Woollen hanks dyed with acid milling dyes*

Plate 6 *Dyeing techniques. Key to outline chart: 1 Various yarns wrapped in cotton cloth and dyed together with hot-water reactive dye; 2 mohair yarn sprayed with acid milling dyes; 3 woollen bouclé yarn sprayed with acid milling dyes; 4 silk yarn sprayed with acid milling dyes; 5 acrylic yarn dip-dyed with disperse dyes*

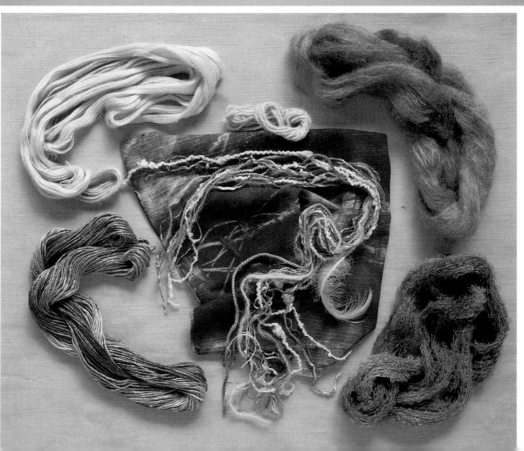

This yarn tended to distort slightly and to fluff, despite care to avoid a rolling boil and to minimise handling when hot and wet. This was the only yarn to be so affected and the result is not unpleasing – the broken surface gives additional reflections that enhance the lustre and impart extra 'life'. Colours were the palest of all, but even and soft.

100% acrylic

This was the only yarn in which the individual fibres had been spun separately and then plied together. In consequence, each retained its own characteristics. Cotton formed the bulk of the yarn with a binder thread of polyester supporting a chenille of acrylic. Cotton does not take disperse dyes to any useful extent and thus remained very pale; the polyester component likewise took little colour as it was dyed by normal processes that did not allow much dye penetration. There was some difference in colour strength between these two fibres resulting in a two-tone twist in a soft pastel tint. The acrylic chenille dyed strongly and introduced splashes of colour at intervals along the yarn, most noticeable in the blue, black, red and violet samples.

*69% cotton/
16% acrylic/
15% polyester*

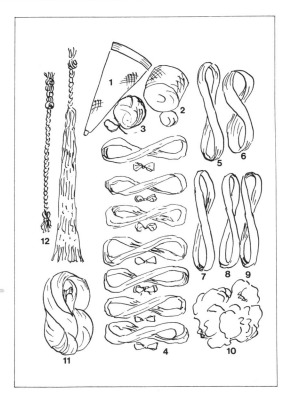

Plate 7 *Different dyeing techniques. Key to outline chart: 1 Cone of silk; 2 ball of woollen yarn; 3 ball of hand-spun Jacob; 4 various coloured and natural yarns. Nos 1–4 all dyed together in acid milling dyes. 5 Silk; 6 wool; 7 linen; 8 cotton/acrylic/polyester; 9 cotton. Nos 5–9 all dyed together in Dylon multi-purpose dye. 10 Fleece dyed in Dylon exhaust; 11 cotton/nylon plied yarn dyed with acid-milling and direct dye; 12 yarn knotted and plaited before dyeing*

60% wool/ 40% acrylic, pre-dyed grey These samples should be compared with the identical fibre dyed on white; the difference shows how basically bright colours can be muted by using a grey or dark fibre, and some interesting effects resulted. Red was changed to crimson, while orange appeared as tan. Yellow united with the components of the original grey dye to produce a subdued yellow/green, while green softened to a pale blue/green. Blue retained its character but became darker, as did violet, but black changed to a rich reddish-brown. All the colours dyed a little unevenly due to the presence on the fibre of the original grey which had partially saturated the fibre molecules, but the effect was pleasing and had more life than a single flat hue.

Disperse dyes are thus a very practical means of colouring man-made fibres obtainable in blends from most retail shops. They could be coloured white to be dyed for the first time, or be already coloured to be over-dyed to yield interesting effects.

10
CHOOSING AND
USING DYES

Most synthetic dyes are made for industrial use and are produced in a good range of colours to reduce the need for mixing as far as possible. A typical pattern card might show around three dozen or so colours and tones. Craft dyers need only a few of these as they can mix any others from a carefully chosen palette – the cost of doing so is not important in a craftroom.

When selecting dyes one needs to understand the system used by manufacturers to describe their products. A pattern card may not always be available for examination, but the strength and colour of a dye can be visualised if one can interpret its description.

First there is a copyrighted brand name indicating the type of dye and its maker – eg 'Procion', which is the registered name for reactive dyes produced by ICI. If there are two or more forms of a dye additional information may be included. Examples of this are 'Procion-MX' and 'Procion-HE', which are cold- and hot-water versions of the ICI reactives.

Next comes the name of the colour, 'yellow', 'red', and so on. There are all sorts of reds and yellows in a variety of mixtures and tones, so the simple name alone does not convey a great deal of information. Colours are more finely described by adding suffix letters to indicate that a basic colour has been modified by the addition of another to alter a tone or hue. For historical reasons the German language is used to identify these additions, the suffix letter 'B' (standing for *blau* in German) indicating the addition of blue, 'G' (*gelb*) the addition of yellow, and 'R' (*rot*) the addition of red. When the letter 'G' is used in connection with a yellow dye, it means the addition of green (*grün*).

The system thus tells us what has been added, but as it stands it does not say how much. This detail is provided by using numbers in addition to the suffix letter. A dye listed as 'Yellow G' is a yellow with some green added; a similar dye with a larger amount of green would be described as 'Yellow 2G', or 'Yellow 3G', and so on. The bigger the number, the greater the amount of additional colour.

The normal production strength of a dye is 100 per cent, and if there is no other indication in its description this is what is implied. If the dye is stronger or weaker than normal an appropriate number is included in its name. A dye shown as 'Yellow 3G 150', for example, would mean it was made to a 150 per cent strength, or 1½ times stronger than normal. When making a 1 per cent solution of such a dye (see Chapter 4, p57) one would use two-thirds of the usual amount of powder or granules. Similarly, a dye with a suffix '50' would be at 50 per cent or half strength, and twice as much would be required to produce a standard 1 per cent stock solution.

A register of dyes has been compiled by the Society of Dyers and Colourists, and lists almost all the seven thousand or so types in current use.

This register, which is called the *Colour Index*, provides information on brand names, colour, fastness, sometimes chemical formulae, and so on. Each dye has its own reference number in the index, and this 'C.I. number', as it is called, provides an exact means of identifying a colour. While the register is intended for use in the dyeing industry, it is significant for craft dyers, especially its information on colour fastness.

Fig 21 *List of recommended dyes*

Recommended Dye	Reasons for Choice
YELLOW: 2G–4G ie, a 'lemon' yellow containing some green	Gives maximum flexibility in use – a lemon yellow can be made into a golden yellow by adding red, but a golden yellow cannot be made into a lemon yellow.
RED: G–3G ie, a yellowish-red, or scarlet	Useful for mixing orange, making browns, 'greying' greens, and producing subtle and dullish purples and violets. On its own it gives salmon pinks at weak strengths.
RED: 3B–6B This is a red with blue in it, such as cerise, bordeaux, magenta, rubine, maroon, etc	When mixed with blue, this red gives clearer and brighter purples and violets than scarlet. Used on its own at weak strengths it gives clear, soft pinks.
BLUE: R or 2R ie, blue with a little red in it such as ultramarine	Makes strong 'holly' greens with yellow, and rich purples with cerise. Used in low strengths with weak reds it gives soft violets and greys.
BLUE: G or 2G, or turquoise ie, blue with a fair amount of green in it	This colour cannot successfully be mixed from other dyes and have the same brilliance. Mixed with yellow it gives very bright greens. With magenta or cerise it produces range of brilliant violets; on its own it is a powerful colour and in low strengths it yields beautiful clear, cool tints.
BLACK: B or 2B ie, black with a little blue in it	Can be used to 'mute' other colours and on its own gives a deep rich hue. Used in low strengths with other weak colours it produces interesting results. With yellow it gives greens and grey-greens; with blue it yields brown-greys, and with reds it gives a range of brick reds.

The statement 'if one has red, yellow, blue and black, one can make all the other colours' is true only to a limited extent. Colours do not all have equal strengths or 'values'; weight for weight, blue is much stronger than orange, for example. Yellow is the weakest of all, with orange, red, green, blue-green, blue and violet following in that order. These differences are important in colour mixing; it may be necessary to blend colours in unequal amounts to obtain an even balance of strength in the mixture.

The nature of a colour is also important and should be considered when choosing dyes that will be used in blends and mixtures. Figs 21 and 22 list the colours that in the experience of the authors may be most useful in assembling a limited palette of dyes. Fig 21 consists of dyes that are recommended as a minimum collection; Fig 22 lists dyes that are not essential but could be useful.

The practical dye palette

Fig 22 *List of additional dyes*

Non-essential but Useful Dye	Reasons for Choice
BROWN: R This is a brown with a little red in it	It is quite possible to mix this colour, but having it ready to hand is more convenient and avoids any risk of 'muddy' results if too many colours are blended together. The brown suggested is more useful than one containing both red and blue as it can be mixed with other colours without 'swamping' them.
GREEN: G to 3G A yellowish-green	This, too, can be mixed but it is convenient to have it ready for use. All greens contain blue, but one with a yellow bias is more flexible in mixing than one with a great deal of blue. A yellow-green can always be 'blued' if required, but a blue-green cannot readily be turned into a yellow-green.

There are two ways of sampling colour mixtures and strengths. One is quick and inexpensive but produces only approximate information, and generally paler colours. The other takes longer and is a little costly in yarn, but yields a comprehensive and invaluable collection of coloured fibre samples for future reference.

Colour sampling

The quick method applies dyes to paper, like paints. White cartridge paper is required, plus a small syringe or eye dropper, a water-colour paint brush, some mixing dishes, stock solutions of dye and a dyeing notebook.

Begin by considering the mixture likely to produce the required colour and estimate the proportions of dye needed, eg a reddish-orange roughly of two parts yellow and one part red. Using the dropper or syringe (the syringe is more accurate) place two drops or measures of yellow on a mixing dish; thoroughly rinse the dropper, then add one drop or measure of red. (The actual amounts used are arbitrary and can be altered as long as the *proportions* remain the same.) Mix the dyes and paint a small area of the cartridge paper, and record the recipe of the sample, viz yellow/scarlet 2:1. Once the dyes have dried the colour balance can be assessed and any adjustments made in the next sample.

This method gives no more than a rough guide and colour strengths may not be accurate, but it is quick and cheap; an index of different dye combinations can be compiled for a modest outlay. The panel at the bottom of Plate 1 shows forty-eight painted samples of the actual dyes used for the yarns in the colour circles above (see also p93, 'The Dye colour circle').

The second technique produces samples by actually dyeing yarn; it takes longer but gives true specimens of colour and a more accurate and permanent record of what was achieved. Yarn is preferred to loose fibre as it is easier to use and file away afterwards.

It is vital to weigh the yarn accurately – any errors will be multiplied when recipes are scaled up for larger amounts of fibre. The smallest measurable amount should be used – probably 5g on kitchen scales – and it should be hanked before dyeing (see Fig 12 and Chapter 4, 'Fibre Preparation'). The hanks do not have to be very long, 12–15cm (5–6in) is quite sufficient. Standard dyeing techniques are followed, as recommended in the chapters on individual dyes. Keep accurate records of each dyeing – colours, amounts, proportions, times, etc – this is vital for reproducing colours in larger scale work later on. Individuals will decide how many samples they wish to produce. The following suggestions are for a reference collection of colours.

First, use each dye on its own but at five colour strengths – 0.1, 0.5, 1, 2 and 3ml/g. This will show how variations in strength affect the tones of a colour (illustrated at the upper half of Plate 2, and noted in Chapter 3, 'Contrast of Tone').

Next, investigate mixtures; begin by adding a constant 0.1ml/g of black to each of the original dyes over all five colour strengths. Note the varying effects black has on the other colours. Try mixtures, using each dye in turn in various proportions with the others; this is a good way of showing relative colour strengths.

Take a look at different yarns, eg wool, silk, mohair, nylon, cotton, and their blends. These might be dyed together in a common bath to show variations in colour take-up by the different fibres and mixtures (illustrated in Plates 3 and 4), and between plied and mixed staple blends (see Chapter 9, 'Fibre Blends').

At the end of the programme there will be a valuable collection of samples to be filed or mounted for reference. There are two methods of doing this:

1 The dyed samples can be knotted in a series of holes punched along one edge of a card. This method (see Fig 23) shows off the texture of the yarn and the way light might affect its colour in loose structures such as knitting, crochet, etc.

2 Alternatively, the yarn could be wrapped around a strip of card as in Plates 1, 2 and 3, to show the samples as they might appear in woven fabrics, tapestry or embroidery. Fig 25 illustrates the method of wrapping.

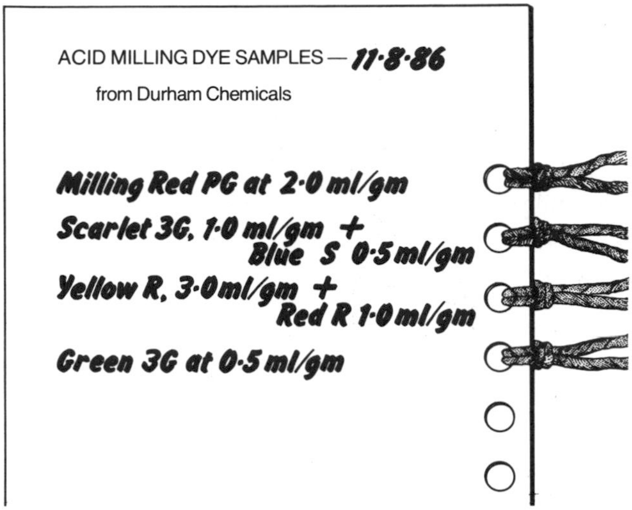

Fig 23 *Mounting
dyed yarn samples
on a punched card*

ACID MILLING DYE SAMPLES — *11·8·86*

from Durham Chemicals

Milling Red PG at 2·0 ml/gm

Scarlet 3G, 1·0 ml/gm +
Blue S 0·5 ml/gm

Yellow R, 3·0 ml/gm +
Red R 1·0 ml/gm

Green 3G at 0·5 ml/gm

Once the samples have been mounted they should be placed on file for easy reference and kept out of direct sunlight.

The dye colour circle

A 'dye' colour circle is a useful tool as it tells one how to mix colours as well as showing how they work together. Plate 1 shows a circle of this type made from worsted yarn dyed with acid milling dyes. It consists of four concentric rings of card wrapped with colour samples; each ring is divided into twelve equal segments to accommodate three primary, three secondary and six intermediate colours (see Fig 24). The outer ring shows tints – dyes used at quarter standard strength; the next is for colours at standard strength – as named in Fig 8; the third ring is for colours also at standard strength but 'shaded' by the addition of their complementaries (see Chapter 3, p36) at half strength. The innermost ring shows colours at half strength, muted by the addition of 0.1ml/g of black in each case. The centre of the circle is dyed with a mixture of red, blue and yellow in varying proportions to produce a suitable tone of grey.

The progression from primary to secondary to intermediate colour shows the effects of colour mixing, while the relative positions of the colours on the circle illustrates harmonies, contrasts, etc.

To make a dye colour circle, the following are required:

○ Two sheets of stout card, at least 380mm (15in) square.
○ A rubber-based glue or double-sided adhesive tape.
○ Suitable yarn – preferably worsted for wool dyes, or mercerised cotton for cellulose dyes.
○ A palette of dyes. The circle in Plate 1 was dyed as described above, from just red, blue, yellow and black.

One sheet of card is divided into four rings by drawing five concentric circles as large as possible and at equal spacings. These rings are divided into twelve equal segments, numbered (see Fig 24), and then cut out. A thin paring of card should be removed from their outer edges to provide room for

Fig 24 *The dye colour circle*

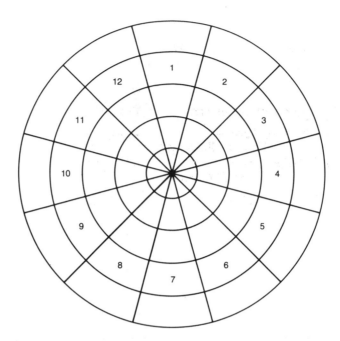

the thickness of the yarn when they are wrapped. The first samples to be made are the primaries red, blue and yellow, which should be dyed to an equal intensity as far as possible. This means that, to compensate for their natural differences in colour value (see p91, 'The Practical Dye Palette'), blue might require to be used at about half the strength of red, but yellow applied at twice its strength.

Wrap these samples around the second largest ('standard') ring locating red at segment 12, yellow at segment 4 and blue at segment 8. One end of the yarn is stuck to the back of the ring with glue or double-sided tape, and the segment then wrapped; each strand should lie closely against its neighbour, especially along the inner edge (see Fig 25). When the segment is full cut the yarn, leaving a tail to be stuck at the back. Record the recipes that were used for the colours – dyes, proportions, etc – and attach a label with this information to any pieces of left-over yarn which will be useful for other experiments.

Dye secondary colours from mixtures of two primaries – red with yellow to produce orange, yellow with blue to give green, and blue with red to make violet. Try to balance these mixtures so that the secondaries are midway in value between their parent primaries. Wrap the samples as before, locating orange on segment 2, green at segment 6 and violet on segment 10. Record the recipes and label the left-over yarn.

Complete the ring by dyeing intermediate colours from mixtures of adjacent primaries and secondaries (see Fig 8), once again balancing their value midway between their parents, as far as possible. These samples are wrapped around the remaining spaces on the ring, in between their parent colours.

When the ring is complete, mount it centrally on the second sheet of card using glue or double-sided tape. Note all the dye proportions that were used

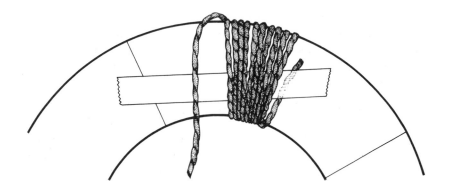

Fig 25 *Wrapping dyed yarn on the colour circle*

to mix each sample, and keep to them in subsequent mixings for the other three rings.

The 'tints' ring is made next, following the same procedure. Use the dyes at reduced strength – say, 0.5ml/g instead of 2ml/g – ie one quarter as strong. Wrap these samples on the outermost ring in the same order as the standard strength colours so that direct comparisons can be made.

Samples for the third – 'shades' – ring are made in the same way, blending colours and mixtures at standard strength with their complementaries at half strength, and using the result at 2ml/g. This will produce a range of full dark shades. Wrap as before in the same order.

Dye colours for the fourth and innermost ring at half strength, and add 0.1ml/g of black in each case. This shows the effect of muting by adding black.

Finish the colour circle by dyeing the centre portion grey. Wrap the yarn around the central disc, which should have a hole cut in its centre to receive it. The four rings and the centre disc should be mounted together on the second sheet of card to make an assembly similar to that shown on Plate 1.

When assessing the results of these experiments, remember the scale of colour values – yellow being weakest and violet strongest. These relationships affect some of the samples on the third – 'shades' – ring of the circle. The natural disproportion in colour strengths means that the complementary colours blue, violet and red used to darken the orange, yellow and green mixtures, have overshadowed the lighter components in the blend and produced an unbalanced result. This is the consequence of using constant proportions when shading with complementaries. If balanced shades are required, giving an even progression of tone from lightest to darkest, it is necessary to use complementaries at a much reduced strength – possibly one quarter – when adding them to the lighter colour mixtures.

Dyed yarn left over from previous experiments can be used to study colour and fibre combinations.

Colour in design studies

1 Twist yarns together and note the effects of plying various colours, or blending them together as in weaving or embroidery. Compare the results at close range and from a distance.

95

2 Yarn that has been dyed to known recipes can be used in colour matching. Coloured photographs, illustrations or even natural objects intended as the basis for designs can be compared with the dyed samples and any changes in colour strength or mixture necessary to achieve a match can be estimated.

3 Wrap yarns to model colour arrangements and proportions for woven hangings, rugs or scarves, or stripes in a sweater, or the colours and textures in an embroidery or tapestry. It is not necessary to confine wrappings to striped patterns; an adhesive on the front of the card will allow yarns to be arranged in curves, or pieces of cut yarn, or dyed fleece or other fibre, to be inset.

4 Unexpected colour schemes may result from these uses of yarn samples. Restful and quiet monochromatic arrangements, or patterns of analogous colours may emerge; if they seem too placid they can be livened up with a touch of a complementary colour.

5 Craftworkers should adopt an adventurous approach to colour, develop confidence in their ability to use it and trust their own judgements. It is not necessary to adhere unswervingly to the sometimes highly technical presentations in various books on the subject, although guidance on more structured colour schemes is available there if required.

6 The foregoing ideas have all considered the use of colour, but the value of black and white and grey should not be forgotten. Colours shown against a black or white background can acquire quite different levels of brilliance and luminosity, while black, white and grey are excellent for separating particularly strong hues and preventing them from clashing with each other.

7 Lighting can have considerable effects on colour, and if ignored can be disastrous: dyes that were carefully chosen in daylight may look completely different under tungsten or fluorescent light. This should be borne in mind when planning a project. Consider the lighting conditions under which it will be seen, and assess sample wrappings, etc in *that* environment.

8 Note that colour matching should never, ever, be attempted in artificial light. Irrespective of where a textile will ultimately be used, colour *matching* – as distinct from colour compatibility – should be undertaken only in daylight. There is a simple reason for this: pigments used in the dyes have absorption characteristics matched to white light and will not reflect the intended wavelengths under other illumination (see Chapter 3, 'Colour in Pigments and Dyes').

These are just a few suggestions the authors have found useful in their own work. We hope they will encourage craftworkers to experiment with dyes and to develop their own individual tastes in colour and design.

11
EXPERIMENTING WITH DYES

When the general principles of dyeing have been understood, one can adapt the procedures by experimenting with new ideas and methods. In this way exciting and unique yarns can be produced for knitting, weaving and embroidery, while spinners can make multi-coloured fibres for blending into yarn, or dip-dye or spray their completed yarns.

Some of these possibilities are now examined, the information being offered as a starting point from which individuals can develop their own innovations and enjoy using and experimenting with dyes.

Yarn can be dip-dyed in different colours, which may be kept separate or overlapped to blend and produce colour mixtures.

Dip-dyeing

○ One dyepot for each colour.
○ Dyeing equipment as required for the dyes being used (see Chapter 4, 'Equipment').
○ Long hanks or lengths of yarn in white or pale colours.
○ Appropriate dyes and assistants.

Equipment and materials

1 Weigh all the yarn and, from this total, estimate the weight of each colour section.

Method

2 Make up dyebaths with appropriate amounts of dye calculated from 1 above. Place the dyepots as close together as possible.

3 Wet the yarn, squeeze out surplus water, and place the parts to be coloured in the appropriate dyebaths. Take great care that the lengths looping from one bath to another are not damaged by heat (see Fig 26).

Fig 26
Arrangements of dyepots and yarn over heat

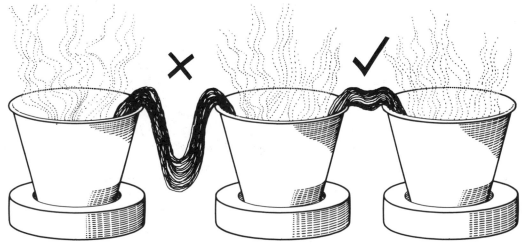

4 Follow normal dyeing procedures (see the relevant chapter), but for overlapping colours (eg yellow blending through green to blue) place more of the yarn in one dyebath than the other. Halfway through the sequence transfer the area to be blended to the second bath. Plate 6, top left hand, shows acrylic yarn dip-dyed in three blending colours by this procedure, using disperse dyes.

5 If separate but adjoining colours are required, wrap plastic strip tightly around the yarn where the second colour is to begin. Dye the first colour and rinse; transfer the wrapping to cover the end of the first colour and then dye the second. Two ends may be dyed at the same time, and then the centre section. This method is especially useful if three differently coloured warps or warp sections are required for a piece of weaving – three scarves or stoles, for example. They could all be woven in one sequence on the length of dyed yarn.

6 A slightly muted effect can be produced by over-dyeing at the end of the dip-dyeing sequence. Calculate the required amount of black or other dye at a strength of, say, 0.1–0.3ml/g. Make a final dyebath with this and over-dye the whole amount of yarn. Watch the process carefully and remove the yarn when the required shade has been obtained.

Spray-dyeing Similar effects to dip-dyeing can be achieved by spraying. The advantages over dip-dyeing are that only one dyebath is required (for fixing the colour); that many more colours can be applied in a given length of yarn; and that dye can be much more closely controlled. The disadvantage is that dyeing must be done out of doors or in a specially protected area indoors, using a shield or box. Strong or muted colours can be produced.

Fig 27 Cardboard box as a spray booth

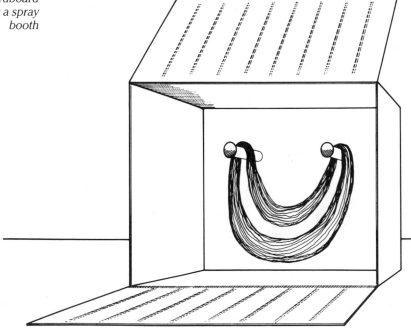

a) Dyeing indoors:
A 'spray booth' is necessary, which can be made from a large cardboard box placed on its side. Locate it near adequate ventilation and protect surrounding wall and table surfaces with newspaper. One end of the box can be cut and folded back to provide a larger spraying area and easier access, but the surrounding surfaces will then need additional protection. Line the box with newspaper to absorb excess spray.

b) Dyeing out-of-doors:
Hanks or lengths of yarn can be draped from a tree branch, nails hammered in a fence or even an up-turned barrow. Wind direction should be checked before spraying or you may finish up being spray-dyed yourself!

For both indoor and outdoor spraying, overalls or a full-length apron with sleeves are necessary, and a facemask is a sensible precaution, especially when using reactive dyes.

Spraying equipment can consist of a plant spray with detachable bottle, or a small compressed-air set.

○ Suitable dyes and appropriate assistants.
○ Hanks or lengths of yarn, or prepared warps.

For wool, silk, mohair; also nylon:

1 Prepare a 1 per cent stock solution of a suitable acid dye (see Chapter 4, 'Dye Solutions').

2 Fill the spray container with the dye solution, using it undiluted for strong colours, but adding a little water for paler tints.

3 Prepare the yarn normally (see Chapter 4, 'Fibre Preparation'). If cut strands are to be sprayed, tie them together at both ends.

4 Soak the yarn for at least 30 minutes in warm water, 40°C (105°F), to which vinegar has been added at a rate of 0.5–1ml/g.

5 After soaking, remove the yarn, squeeze out surplus water, and arrange it in the spray booth. Small sticks or dowels can be pushed through from the back to support it (see Fig 27). Use newspaper to mask off sections that are not meant to be coloured.

6 Warp threads may require special treatment, and be better stretched out flat for more accurate placing of dye than bunched. In this case thin card makes a better mask than newspaper because it can be cut to an intricate shape according to a pattern. It can be fixed with double-sided tape. Be careful when spraying a warp that dye does not penetrate behind the masking – plastic and paper beneath the yarn will protect its under-surface.

7 Spray as required, turning yarn if necessary to colour its reverse side; most of its surface should be covered with dye. Remove masks during colour changes and replace them with fresh paper or card to cover new areas.

Change the paper lining of the booth each time a new length of yarn is to be dyed.

8 To fix the colour, prepare a fairly wide-bottomed bath with enough water almost to cover the yarn. Add vinegar at 0.5ml/g and heat the liquor to roughly 60°C (140°F). Place the yarn gently in this bath and slowly increase the temperature to boiling point (for wool, mohair and nylon), or 80°C (175°F) for silk. Maintain this heat for 20 minutes, then cool, rinse and soap the yarn as normal (see Chapter 4, 'Soaping'). Some colour will be lost from wool and mohair, but not from silk which readily absorbs the dye.

Plate 6, right side, top and bottom, and left side, bottom only, shows mohair, wool and silk in that order, all dyed by the spraying technique.

Method For cotton, linen, etc:

1 Prepare a solution of cold-water reactive dye, using a 1 per cent strength for pale tints but a 5 per cent concentration for full colours. Urea is used to help dissolve the 5 per cent solution (see Chapter 4, 'Dye Solutions' and 'Dyebath Assistants').

2 Prepare the yarn in the usual way (see Chapter 4, 'Fibre Preparation').

3 Make a solution of washing soda as directed in Chapter 4, 'Dyebath Assistants'. This allows the dye to react and fix on the yarn, and it can be applied in two ways:

a) It can be added to a soaking bath in the ratio of 1:10, and the yarn immersed in this liquor for 30 minutes before spraying. The strongest colours are obtained by this method.
b) It can be poured over the coloured yarn after spraying. This is the easier method but it produces paler colours.

Plate 9 shows examples of both techniques. The hank at extreme top left was dyed at 1 per cent and the one next to it at 5 per cent, and both had soda poured over them after dyeing. The hank at bottom right was pre-soaked in soda before being dyed at 5 per cent. The differences are clear.

4 Ensure the yarn is well wetted, squeeze out surplus moisture, and arrange it for spraying in the booth as before, either as a bunched hank or a spread warp. After spraying, allow the yarn to dry naturally before setting the colour.

5 There are three ways of setting the dye:

a) The yarn can be left in a warm place for at least 48 hours, during which time the dye/fibre reaction will be completed.
b) It can be heated with a hair-drier to speed up the reaction; 10–15 minutes are normally sufficient.
c) It can be baked in an electric (not gas because of its open flame) oven at a temperature not above 140°C (285°F). It must be kept well clear of the sides and heating elements, and should be baked for 5–10 minutes only, ensuring it does not overheat.

6 After baking, the yarn is rinsed and soaped by normal procedures (see Chapter 4, 'Soaping').

In these notes we have suggested newspaper or thin card for masking. There are proprietary resist agents sold for this purpose, but they are mainly intended for fabric or paper and cannot be recommended for yarns. In the authors' experience they are almost impossible to remove.

Yarn can be painted with thickened dye – a technique especially useful for colouring warps. Acid dyes at 1–5 per cent strength are used for wool and silk, and reactive dyes at 5 per cent for cotton and linen. Fabric also can be coloured by this process.

Painting with dyes

○ An oil-colour paint brush.
○ A fairly wide vessel for a soaking bath.
○ An old kitchen steamer or pressure cooker.

Equipment

○ Acid or reactive dyes.
○ Urea.
○ Manutex.
○ Soda solution.

Materials

For all fibres and dyes:

Preparation

1 Make dye solutions to an appropriate strength, bearing in mind that although colours may appear strong they will be softened in weaving. Use urea to help dissolve the dye powders, and Manutex to thicken the solutions (see Chapter 4, 'Dye Solutions' and 'Dyebath Assistants').

2 Prepare the yarn (see Chapter 4, 'Fibre Preparation') and stretch it between pegs or over a table. In the case of warps, insert cross-sticks and spread open the ends. Mark any designs with a soft pencil or dressmaker's pen, and protect areas beneath with newspaper or plastic sheeting.

For wool and silk:

Method

1 Add vinegar to acid dye mixtures at a rate of 1ml for each 10ml of dye.

2 Ensure the yarn is dry and then paint on the dye, dabbing downwards to ensure it penetrates the yarn. Allow each area to dry before colouring adjacent areas, unless blurred outlines or colour mixtures are required.

3 After the dyes have dried, remove the yarn from the pegs, etc; in the case of warps, remove the cross-sticks and replace with yarn, retying the end loops. The yarn now has to be steamed to set the dye. Fold it in kitchen foil as shown in Fig 28 so that it is totally enclosed, and coil it into a circular package.

4 There are three ways of steaming:

a) In a large pan; the yarn package is placed on an upturned bowl to keep it above the water, and steamed for an hour.

b) In a steamer; the package should be placed centrally away from the sides and water, and steamed for an hour.

c) In a pressure cooker, placed centrally and away from water, and steamed for 15–20 minutes.

Fig 28 Painted yarns folded into foil for steaming

Plate 9 shows two painted wool warps at its centre. The upper specimen was dyed at 1 per cent strength, and the lower at 5 per cent. Both were set by steaming in a pressure cooker.

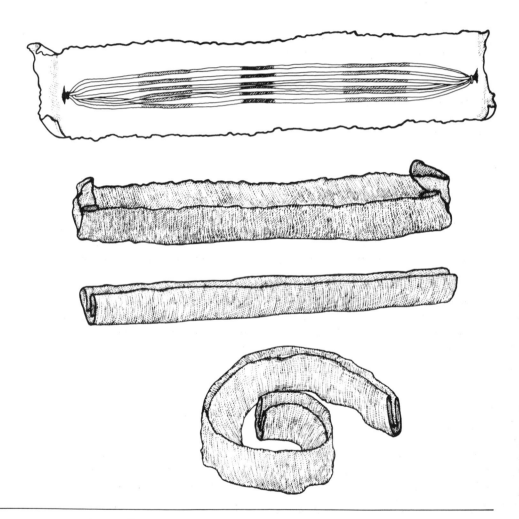

Plate 8 *Ikat.* (Top) *Sample hanks and dyed weft yarn.* (Centre) *Wrapped warp strips in various stages.* (Bottom) *Completed ikat sections as on the loom.*

Plate 9 *Painting and spraying techniques. Cotton hanks sprayed at various dye strengths. Woollen warps painted at 1 per cent and 5 per cent strength*

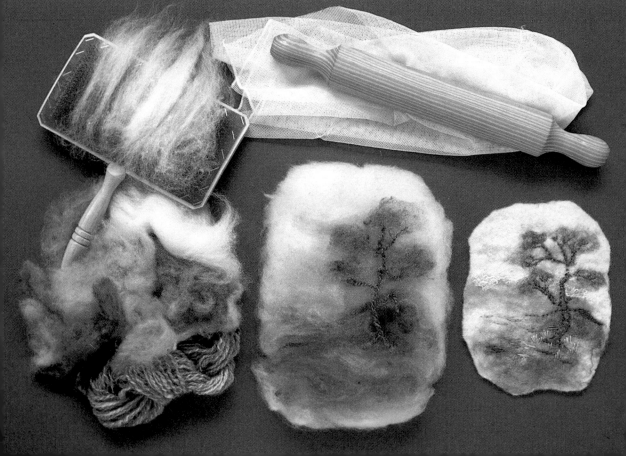

For cotton and linen: *Method*

1 Add soda solution (see Chapter 4, 'Dyebath Assistants') to a soaking bath in the ratio 1:10, and immerse the yarn in this liquor for 30 minutes. Allow it to dry without rinsing or squeezing, and then stretch it between pegs or over a table as previously described.

2 Paint on the dye as directed for wool and silk yarns, ensuring that the threads are completely encircled with paint.

3 The dye now has to be set. Allow the paint to dry and then use one of the setting processes for cotton or linen, described under 'Spray-dyeing'.

Warps can also be painted on the loom – a technique that allows colour to be placed exactly where required with no risk of subsequent disturbance. Yarn is prepared as previously described and then wound on the loom (which must be well protected). The exposed section is painted and allowed to dry before the warp is wound forward to expose the next area. This sequence is repeated until colouring is complete; the warp is then rewound on the back roller in readiness for weaving. When the fabric is finished it is removed from the loom and treated appropriately to fix the dye.

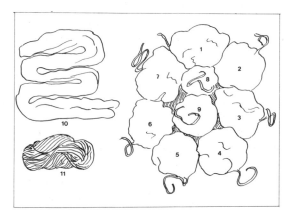

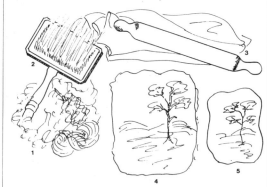

Plate 10 *Dyed fibres and rainbow-dyed roving.*
Key to outline chart:
1 Terylene with disperse dye;
2 tussah silk with acid milling dye;
3 alpaca with acid levelling dye;
4 samoyed dog with acid-milling dye;
5 mohair with acid metal-complex dye;
6 angora rabbit with acid metal-complex dye;
7 cotton with cold-water reactive dye;
8 nylon with disperse dye;
9 ramie with hot-water reactive dye;
10 silk/alpaca roving rainbow-dyed with acid
milling dyes;
11 hand-spun yarn produced from 10 above

Plate 11 *Felt.*
Key to outline chart:
1 Natural and dyed fleece and yarns;
2 batt on carder;
3 nylon netting and rolling-pin;
4 prepared fleece batts with design;
5 completed felt with added embroidery

Over-dyeing While it is usual to dye only white or grey yarns and fibres, interesting and unusual effects can be obtained by over-dyeing on coloured materials. A knowledge of colour mixing is useful when considering the effect one dye will have on another – for example, red applied to a yellow yarn will predictably make an orange, but on grey the result would be a muted red, and on green it would produce a brown.

Balls of yarn, cops and cones can be given a new interest by over-dyeing, while oddments of differently coloured yarn too small and dissimilar for use on their own can be colour co-ordinated for a new lease of life together.

The centre column of Plate 7 shows the results of over-dyeing a cone and a ball of yarn, a ball of hand-spun Jacob, and a selection of differently coloured yarns, all with scarlet acid dye at 1.5ml/g. The miniature hanks between the larger ones show the yarns in their original colours.

Method **1** Estimate the amount of dye required. For the best results use fairly strong and bright colours. Balls of hand-spun Jacob or other coloured fleece can be dyed very effectively with bright colours like scarlet, turquoise and violet.

2 Make a dyebath as appropriate for the type of fibre and dye.

3 Immerse balls, cops and cones of yarn while they are dry, but ensure hanks are well wetted first (see Chapter 4, 'Fibre Preparation'). Follow the appropriate dyeing procedures as specified in the relevant dye chapters.

4 After dyeing, finish hanks as directed in the relevant dye chapters. Balls, cops and cones should be partly unwound and inspected; flecks of their original colour will progressively appear until a point is reached where all signs of the over-dye are lost. The yarn can be redyed from this point if required, repeating the procedure.

Another form of over-dyeing was described in the American magazine *Handwoven*, Vol 5, No 3 (Interweave Press, 1984). Although this was meant for natural dyes it is equally effective with synthetic compounds. Different types and colours of yarn and fibre are wrapped in a piece of fabric and tied tightly; the bundle is immersed in an appropriate dyebath and the normal procedures carried out. The fibres will take the dye selectively, while the fabric will have a tie-dyed appearance; the whole bundle will be colour co-ordinated and its contents can be used together with good effect – for an embroidery, for example.

The centre portion of Plate 6 shows an example of this technique. Hot-water reactive dyes – 1.75ml/g of red and 0.3ml/g of turquoise – were used to colour a variety of wool, cotton and man-made yarns, and even a feather, all wrapped in a cotton/linen fabric. The results show the degree of colour harmony that can be achieved.

Attractively flecked yarns can be produced by over-dyeing coloured yarn while it is plaited or knotted. When it is undone after dyeing it shows a pattern of variegated colouring that enhances knitting, weaving or embroidery. An example is presented in Plate 7, top left. The left specimen of the pair is plaited and knotted and seen immediately after over-dyeing; the right-hand sample has been undone to show the two-colour effect.

Rainbow-dyeing originated in America as a method of colouring fleece; it is now a well-established technique equally suitable for woollen, silk or hair yarns. Different dyes are used at the same time and applied randomly without precise measurement to create a multi-coloured 'rainbow' effect. In the original procedure the dyes were sprinkled as dry powders, and this method is still sometimes encountered. The authors believe this is unwise because of the possibility of dusts being created and inhaled. The recommended alternative is to apply the dyes as liquids, made up as normal 1 per cent stock solutions (see Chapter 4, 'Dye Solutions'). Dyes of the acid group (see Chapter 5) are normally used, and in applying them the differences in relative colour strength should be borne in mind (see Chapter 10, 'The Practical Dye Palette') and quantities balanced accordingly.

Rainbow-dyeing

○ Dyepot, preferably with a broad base, and large enough to contain fibres.
○ Aluminium foil to cover the dyepot.

Equipment

○ Stock solutions of dye.
○ Vinegar.
○ Detergent (for unwashed fleece).

Materials

For wool and hair fibres:

Method

1 Place enough water in the dyepot to wet the fleece or yarn without covering it or allowing it to float.

2 Add vinegar at approximately 0.5ml/g.

3 If unwashed fleece is being dyed, add detergent at 0.2ml/g.

4 Place the fibres in the dyepot. Fleece and rovings can be entered dry, but yarn should be wetted first so that dye liquor can more easily penetrate its tighter structure. Fleece should be arranged with the tips of the staple pointing down. Yarns and rovings can be arranged randomly or coiled, or doubled to and fro (see Fig 29) to produce an irregular or repeating pattern of colours.

Fig 29 Distribution of dye on rovings or yarns

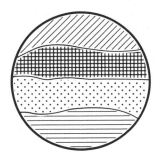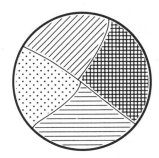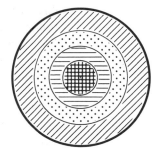

5 Warm the dyebath slightly, then pour or squirt on the dyes (depending on their container) where required. Fleece can be coloured randomly or to a pattern (see Fig 30). A little black dye, diluted to half strength and applied in small amounts over the top of the fibres, will soften the colours.

Fig 30 *Distribution of dye on fleece*

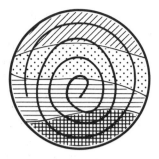

6 Gently push the fibres down with a stirring rod to allow the dye to penetrate them, but do not otherwise stir or move them.

7 Cover the dyepot with a lid or perforated foil and *slowly* heat to simmering; continue to dye at that temperature for about 30 minutes.

8 When dyeing is complete allow the bath to cool slightly and then carefully lift out the fibres with the minimum of disturbance, and rinse them in hot water. Fleece should be rinsed several times and then placed in an old pillowcase prior to a light spin. The fibres can be dried away from direct heat; fleece should be teased out before drying.

After dyeing, there will be some liquor remaining. This can be used to colour more fleece which can then be spun into a singles yarn for plying with a rainbow-dyed yarn. Add a little more vinegar, water if necessary, and a small amount of fleece; cover the dyepot and simmer for 30–40 minutes, then finish as before.

Method For silk fibres:

Silk in the forms of mawata cap, throwsters waste, silk tops, cut silk tops and yarn, may all be rainbow-dyed. The method is the same as for wool except that little or no vinegar is used, and the dyebath temperature should never rise above low simmering (steam just becoming visible). After dyeing, silk is finished in the same way as wool but must be handled with great care.

Examples of rainbow-dyeing are shown in Plate 4, where metal complex dyes were used, and in Plate 10, for which acid milling dyes were chosen.

At the centre of Plate 4 a Wensleydale fleece has been rainbow-dyed as described; the hank on its left was spun from it. The dark roving below is grey New Zealand Romney, coloured by the same method and wound to and fro in the dyepot to produce a regular pattern. A hank of silk is shown above the fleece, and a hank of mohair to its right; both of these were mixed in with the fleece for dyeing.

Plate 10, top left, shows a silk/alpaca roving arranged as it was in the dyepot, and coloured with acid milling dyes. The hank beneath shows it spun into a yarn and plied.

Colour variety in yarns Spinners can make interesting and uniquely coloured yarns by blending fibres during carding, or carefully choosing colours when plying, or by using fibres that have been especially coloured for an effect. Similarly, dyers can

108

colour commercial multifibre yarns or hand-spun yarns made from different fibres to take advantage of their varying reactions to dyes.

The following ideas are offered as a starting point for individual experiment and exploration.

Carding

Differently coloured fibres can be blended together by carding. If they are teased out and very well carded, the result will be a softly coloured, even mixture, similar to the 'lovat' hues. With light carding the fibres will be less well mixed and individual colours will be visible, giving extra life to a yarn; fairly bright colours give the best results.

The appearance of a yarn is also affected by the arrangement of the fibres on the carders. It is worth experimenting with strips of coloured fibre placed in even and uneven arrangements, both with and without contrasting 'base' fibres; keep a note of such arrangements so that they can be repeated and a consistent yarn produced.

Different – as well as differently coloured – fibres can be blended by carding to enhance the appearance of a yarn (see Plate 10, right side). Their texture and lustre can be used to highlight a colour combination and give it extra life (see Chapter 3, 'Colour and Texture'). Beware when mixing coloured fibres, as in all colour mixing, not to create muddy shades by using too many complementary colours.

Plying

Singles yarns in different colours can be plied to produce a striped effect. The stridency of this will depend upon contrast; analogous colours will yield quietly beautiful results, but strongly differing colours can give loud results. Seen at close range the individual colours in a plied yarn may be obvious, but from a distance the effect is more likely to be a blend of them; this should be borne in mind when colours are selected. As an alternative to plying two colours, one colour can be folded with a natural white or grey yarn – this will produce soft natural blends especially attractive in knitting and crochet.

Variegated yarns

Slivers of rainbow-dyed roving or tops can be spun as variegated singles, and two such yarns plied together will create an even more interesting result. Similar effects can be obtained by spinning from a sequence of differently coloured rolags, and plying the result by the Navajo method – a technique described in many spinning books – to keep the colours separate.

Brightening yarns

A great variety of tints and shades can be made by using strongly coloured fibres in different proportions with natural white, grey, brown or black fleece or fibre. In the same way, a touch of peacock blue, scarlet or emerald can bring life and vivacity to a dark fleece like a Jacob. Tiny pieces of contrasting yarn or felted fleece can be introduced when spinning or plying to create an interesting nep yarn.

Ideas are almost endless, and if notes and samples are kept of various experimental results, a useful record can be built up to allow any successes to be repeated.

Multifibre Many commercial yarns are available in multifibre combinations mixed
yarns either as chopped and blended staple, or as individual plies. Similar hand-
spun yarns can be produced by carding different fibres together, or blending
them while spinning, or plying them as individual singles. Dyeing these
yarns can be an interesting exercise: single dyes can be chosen that will
colour just one fibre, or two differing dyes can be used to colour both fibres.
Some dyes can be mixed and used together in a common dyebath, and if
they are of different colours, a two-colour yarn can be produced by one
dyeing process. It is thus possible to produce a yarn of which part is
coloured and part not, or one with two colours blended together, or a striped
yarn if the two fibres are plied.

Mixtures of dye types are limited by their compatibilities, and one of the
best combinations is a direct dye used simultaneously with an acid dye.
Other possibilities are direct and disperse dyes for nylon/cotton mixtures, or
reactive and disperse dyes for polyester/cotton blends. Some of the
proprietary household dyes perform similarly to the all-purpose or union
dyes that are a mixture of a conventional acid and a direct, and are intended
to colour wool, nylon and cotton fibres by a substantially common process.

Tests were carried out to investigate the performance of the Dylon dye of
this type. Two dyebaths were prepared as instructed, and half the intended
weight of fibre was added to each, wool in one and cotton in the other. The
recommended dyeing cycle was followed, then the fibres were removed,
rinsed and dried. Further salt was added to the baths together with fresh
fibre – cotton where wool was before, and vice versa. After the prescribed
cycle these fibres, too, were rinsed and dried.

Comparing the two dyeings, fibre with fibre, showed no differences in
colour strength. It was apparent that dye taken up by the first set of fibres
was not absorbed to the detriment of the second. The conclusion is that if a
bath of this type of dye is used to colour just one kind of fibre, only the part
of the dye related to that fibre will be taken up; the rest will remain unused,
either to be thrown away, or to remain available to colour other fibre in due
course. To prove this conclusion a third dyebath was loaded as prescribed,
with wool, cotton, linen, silk and an acrylic/cotton/terylene fibre. The silk
coloured much more strongly than the wool, and both took up more dye
than the others, but colour strengths were perfectly adequate to support the
previous conclusion.

After these tests it was noticed that the spent liquor in the dyebath seemed
still to have a good colour, so it was recharged again with salt and a further
load of fibre added – this time in the form of washed fleece. It, too, coloured
to a very good strength, indicating that an exhaust bath of these dyes is well
worth exploiting even though the tones may not be repeatable.

Further experiments showed that it is possible to mix these proprietary
dyes with ordinary direct dyes to obtain a wider range of colours than those
marketed.

Experimental dyeings were also carried out on a plied commercial nylon/
cotton yarn, using a blue direct dye at 0.5ml/g and a brown acid milling dye
at 1ml/g. Each dye was first used on its own to colour part of the fibre
mixture, and then both together in the same dyebath. Plate 7, bottom left

corner, shows the three results, wound together for reasons of space into a single hank. The direct dye coloured the cotton part of the yarn quite strongly but had only a staining effect on the nylon. The acid dye gave a rich colour on the nylon but scarcely any on the cotton. When both dyes were used together the whole yarn was coloured in the two hues which were slightly darker than when dyed singly.

The results from the Dylon tests are also shown on the photograph by the turquoise specimens at the right. Top are the silk and wool hanks; below them, the linen, mixed fibre and cotton samples. At the bottom is the fleece that was dyed in the 'exhaust' bath.

Proprietary stripping compounds are intended to remove colour from the whole of an article or garment in preparation for dyeing in another colour, but they can also be used on yarns and fibres to produce a variety of results. These effects are a matter of dye chemistry and they depend upon the nature of the original dyes; experiments should always be undertaken first if this technique is to be used for a large-scale project. Nevertheless, the use of a stripping agent offers these benefits: **Stripping dyes for colour change**

○ A space-dyed effect can be created with just one original dyeing and no wrapping.
○ Two tones of a colour can be obtained from one dyeing.
○ Colours can be changed to produce two-coloured yarns.

Plate 5 shows the results of using Dygon (Dylon International) on hanks of cotton yarn coloured with cold-water reactive dyes (left) and woollen yarn coloured with acid milling dyes (right). Only a half of each hank was stripped, the original colours appearing in the centre of the illustration.

Blue, and colours containing blue, gave the most unexpected results. They lost colour in the stripping bath but upon exposure to air it redeveloped – as it does when dyeing with indigo. With turquoise the tone became lighter, but the acid ultramarine changed to a green/brown. Reds and colours containing a good deal of red such as brown and violet, stripped to a lighter tone that could be used as it was, or redyed to another colour. Acid yellow stripped very little, but its reactive counterpart lost most of its colour.

These tests illustrate the need for sample stripping to find out what will happen, but they also demonstrate the variations that can be made in the colour of yarns for extremely modest outlays of time, trouble and cost. The results would be very useful in knitting, weaving and embroidery.

○ Dyepot. *Equipment*

○ Proprietary stripping agent. *Materials*

1 Measure out the stripping agent as directed in the manufacturer's instructions, and add it to water in the dyepot. For the tests with Dygon, a teaspoonful was used for roughly 100g (4oz) of yarn. *Method*

111

2 Lower the part of the yarn to be stripped into the solution and apply gentle heat. Leave it until a satisfactory colour has been obtained; this may take a few minutes, or it may be necessary to increase the temperature to boiling and then to simmer for 10 minutes – it all depends on the dye.

3 When stripped, remove the yarn, rinse, wash, rinse and dry away from direct heat.

The reducing agent sodium dithionite (see Chapter 4, 'Dyebath Assistants') can be used instead of a proprietary compound. When stripping cotton yarns, add one level teaspoonful of each of sodium dithionite and ordinary washing soda to the dyepot; for wool, add a teaspoonful of each of dithionite and ammonia. Then proceed as before.

Tests with this method produced similar results to those from Dygon, but cotton yarn dyed orange with a direct dye, stripped to a burgundy that changed to violet upon exposure to air.

Dyeing in a microwave oven

Microwave heating is used in commercial dyehouses to reduce process times and save costs. A domestic microwave oven can be used in the same way and is especially useful when only small amounts of yarn are to be dyed – for an embroidery project, for example. The fibres can be coloured easily and without assembling and using all the equipment normally required for dyeing. The following process is suitable for various types of yarn and hot-water dyes.

Equipment

○ Microwave oven – this will not be contaminated by dye and can still be used for food preparation.
○ Microwave-safe bowl or beaker, reserved for dyeing only, or plastic 'Boil-a-Bags' suitable for use in a microwave. Bags allow a number of small samples to be dyed simultaneously, but they must be supported upright in the oven.

Materials

○ Appropriate dyes and dyebath assistants (see relevant chapters).
○ Clingfilm or microwave-safe plastic film to cover the dyepot. Note that while this material is suitable for dyeing activities, it should not be used when cooking food.

Method

1 Add water to the chosen container at a liquor ratio of 20:1, ensuring that the vessel will still accommodate it when it boils up.

2 Add the dyes and dyebath assistants, then the wetted fibre or yarn, and stir.

3 Cover bowls or beakers with a plate or plastic film, perforating the latter to allow steam to escape. Boil-a-Bags should be loosely secured at the neck with string or an elastic band, but *never* metal ties. Perforate the necks if necessary to allow steam to escape.

4 Set the oven to 'high' until the liquid boils and then reduce to 'medium' or 'simmer' for a further 5–10 minutes. The exact time will depend upon the amount of fibre being coloured; a 10g test hank (200ml dyebath) took approximately 2 minutes to boil. If a number of samples are being dyed simultaneously, extra time will be needed for heating and simmering.

5 After dyeing, allow the fibre to cool in the container, then rinse, wash, rinse and dry, as normal.

6 Boil-a-Bags can be washed after dyeing for reuse.

Rainbow-dyeing can also be carried out in a microwave oven. Place small amounts of yarn or fibre in a suitable bowl or dish with appropriate amounts of water and vinegar. Sprinkle on the dye solutions, cover the container and proceed as previously described. Differing tones of a colour can be dyed at the same time; make up one fairly strong dye solution and use part at full strength, and other parts progressively diluted with water in set proportions.

Dyeing in a pressure cooker

Because of the limited size of a domestic pressure cooker and the need to ensure that the safety valve remains unobstructed, only small amounts of fibre can be dyed at a time. It is a quick and simple way of dyeing, however, and especially valuable if temperatures above boiling point are required (see Chapter 9). As the dye liquor will be in contact with the cooker it must not be used for food, but reserved exclusively for dyeing.

Equipment

○ Pressure cooker, preferably able to generate approximately 15 psi pressure.

Materials

○ Appropriate dyes and dyebath assistants (see relevant chapter).

Method

1 Add water to the cooker at a 30:1 liquor ratio.

2 Add the dyes and dyebath assistants, then the wetted fibres or yarn.

3 Bring the cooker up to pressure and process for 10 minutes.

4 Allow the cooker to cool naturally – do not cool it quickly under a cold tap. When it is cool, relieve any remaining pressure and remove the fibre.

5 Finish by rinsing, washing, rinsing and drying, as normal.

Using dyed fibres for felt

Oddments of dyed fleece and yarn left over from dyeing and spinning experiments can be used up in felt-making – for a garment, footwear, hat, bag or a simple felt picture. As the basic procedures are similar for each, a simple picture has been chosen as an example, the main stages being illustrated in Plate 11.

Any reader who wishes to explore felt-making more deeply is directed to other books on the subject, some of which are included in the Bibliography.

Equipment   ○ Rubber gloves.
  ○ Nylon netting (old curtains will do).
  ○ A rolling-pin.
  ○ A large seed tray, photographic dish or something similar.
  ○ A needle and dark thread.
  ○ Carders.
  ○ A crêpe bandage (useful but not vital).

Materials   ○ Washed white or grey fleece.
  ○ Various portions of coloured fleece.
  ○ Hand-spun yarn.
  ○ Embroidery yarns.

Method   **1** Card the fleece, leaving it as flat batts if hand carders are used. Dyed fleece may be blended with white, grey or other colours, to produce varied effects.

2 Plan the finished size of the felt, allowing for some shrinkage during the process. Lay the carded batts on one half of the nylon netting, overlapping them slightly (see Fig 31). When the required size is reached, make a second layer at right angles to the first, and then a third running in the same direction as the first. More criss-cross layers can be added for really thick felt.

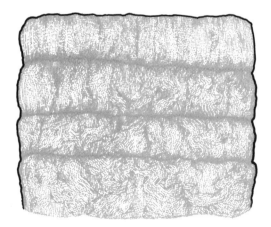 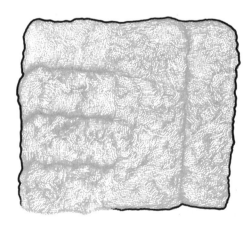

Fig 31 *Building up fleece batts for felting*

3 Pieces of coloured fleece, teased out or carded, are now added to form a design, with other fibres like silk, mohair or alpaca, if required. Hand-spun yarn can be partly untwisted and formed into the shape of a tree, while chopped pieces of coloured yarn and fleece can be added to give an impression of flowers or bushes, etc.

4 When the design is complete, gently fold over the other half of the netting and tack round the edges with fairly large stitches, making sure they go through to the back. For added security, the package can be stitched diagonally as well (see Fig 32).

5 Heat, moisture, pressure and agitation are required for the felting process

114

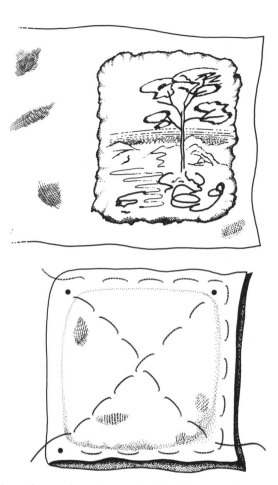

Fig 32 *Building up the pattern with dyed fleece and yarn*

to take place. Place the package in a suitable sink or container, sprinkle on a small amount of detergent or soap flakes and pour on a little very hot water. Wearing rubber gloves, gently press down on the package with the palms of the hands, and later with the knuckles. Keep pressing and pummelling for at least 15 minutes until the fleece begins to adhere together. Turn the package round while working and also over on to the other side. As the water cools, pour it off and add more hot with a little more detergent as a lubricant.

6 When the piece feels reasonably firm, remove it from the netting and wrap it around the rolling-pin; the bandage can be used to secure it. Roll the pin to and fro over an old wash-board or a grooved draining-board, changing the position of the felt from time to time so that it 'fulls' or thickens equally in all directions. Note that felting will take place in the direction of the rolling. This stage should also take about 15 minutes.

7 After sufficient fulling, remove the felt from the rolling-pin and rinse it several times in warm water, then spin lightly and finally dry flat away from direct heat.

8 The design on the felt can now be accentuated with a few embroidery stitches to pick out highlights and give a slightly quilted effect.

Plate 11 shows stages in the creation of a felt picture. Typical materials are grouped in the bottom left corner; above them fleece is being carded into a batt. At the bottom centre a pastoral scene has been assembled from pieces of coloured fleece, teased out hand-spun yarn, etc, ready for enclosure in the netting above, and felting. At the bottom right corner the same design is shown in its completed, felted form. Note the shrinkage that has occurred.

Ikat Ikat is the centuries-old craft of tying and dyeing yarns before weaving. Although its origins are unknown, its name comes from the Malay-Indonesian word *mengikat*, meaning 'to tie'; the same technique is called *kasuri* in Japan from the verb *kasureru*, 'to blur'. The art has been practised for very many years in other countries as well – South America, West Africa and India, but it is said to be most highly developed in Indonesia. Although ikat is historically important, it has been placed last in this chapter because it is a detailed technique, and requires more planning, time and experience than most of the other processes that have been described.

The art involves binding yarns before they are dyed, thus creating uncoloured or 'resist' areas which are then used to produce a two-colour pattern in weaving. Multi-coloured patterns can also be made by repeating the process. When the yarns are wound on the loom, slight displacement of the threads creates the characteristic 'watery' appearance. The warp can be left undisturbed so that the ikat sections appear as squares or rectangles, or the threads may be pulled to create diagonal or arrowhead designs (see Fig 33). The resist areas may be produced in the warp alone, or in the weft alone, or in both warp and weft together; the more intricate designs are produced by the latter method.

Fig 33 *Ikat pattern variations*

Obviously, careful planning is necessary, and it is sensible first to work out a colour scheme on paper. Some idea of colour mixing will help avoid muddy colours if any over-dyeing is required, and a few sample dyeings will show the effect one colour may have on another. Fig 34 was used when planning a four-colour ikat shown in Plate 8, and discussed later; it gives a

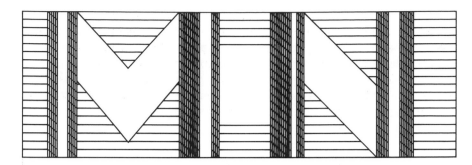

Fig 34 *Ikat planning diagram*

good idea of what is involved. Ikat may be placed as a narrow strip in a garment, or in wider bands, and for the best effect it is usual to combine it with plain colour stripes, as in Plate 8. These also need to be included in the planning and in the warp preparation. The following instructions are for two-colour ikat warp strips, and they assume that the reader has some experience in dressing a loom, and in weaving.

○ Warping posts and clamps, or a warping frame.   *Equipment*
○ Scissors.
○ Dyeing equipment.

○ Dyes and dyebath assistants as appropriate.   *Materials*
○ Yarn for the warp and weft threads.
○ Cotton for the warp ties.
○ Plastic strip or raffia for wrapping.
○ Pencil or washable ballpoint for marking the warp.

1 Using white yarn, make a warp divided into strips, each wide enough for a   *Method* part of the ikat pattern. Treat each strip separately, using a single cross at each end and tying each end loop tightly; attach further ties at intervals of about ½m (½yd) along the warp. Secure the crosses with ties, and if required count the threads for raddling. Wind any plain sections of the warp and treat them in the same way. To identify the order of the strips of warp, tie a plastic tag at the back of each of them (see Fig 35). These can be home-made from old plastic containers, and notched to show the number of each warp section.

2 Remove the warp from the posts or frame and weigh it.

3 It is easiest to wrap a warp while it is under tension, so it should now be replaced on its pegs, or stretched out between two tables or chairs. Sit in a comfortable position and mark all the sections to be wrapped, using a dress-making pen or a pencil, which will wash out later. Mark all the sections before wrapping to be sure of exact measurements. Two or more identical strips can be wrapped together and separated after dyeing, provided the bundle is not too thick; if it is, dye will seep under the bindings.

4 A special tape is available for wrapping, but raffia will do as well or 1cm

Fig 35 *Plastic tag for warp*

117

(½in) strips cut from plastic refuse bags. Begin at the left-hand side of the marked area, leaving a loose end, and wrap tightly to cover the warp to the end of the section. Now reverse the wrapping back to the beginning and tie the two ends with a half bow; if the short end is cut to about 2cm (¾in), and the long end that formed the loop of the bow to about 4cm (1½in), it will be easy to find and pull the correct piece when dyeing is complete, and thus remove the wrapping without using scissors (see Fig 36).

Fig 36 *Wrapping an ikat strip*

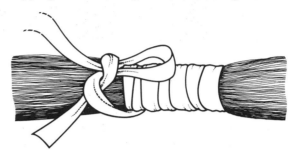

5 After wrapping, make hanks for the weft yarn if it, too, is to be dyed.

6 Estimate the amount of yarn that is to be dyed, including ikat sections and any plain strips, and calculate its weight by reference to the total weight measured at stage 2. Weigh any weft yarn to be dyed, and add this to the total. A typical calculation might look like this:

Weight of ikat sections	60g
Weight of plain strips in warp	20g
Weight of weft yarn to be dyed	80g
	160g

From this answer work out the amount of dye solution required at a rate of, say, 2ml/g. From the figures in the example, the answer would be 320ml.

7 To prevent dye liquor seeping under the wrappings, place cotton and linen warps in a bath of cold water and bring them slowly up to simmering, and simmer for about 15 minutes. Woollen and silk warps are placed in hot water, 60°C (140°F), for 15 minutes, and then allowed to cool. In both cases dyeing then follows normally (see relevant chapters) followed by rinsing and washing, etc (see Chapter 4, 'Soaping').

8 The wrappings only are now removed, all other ties being left in, and the warp allowed to dry. Refer to the plastic tags and arrange the warp sections in order on the back rod of the loom; insert cross-sticks, place the warp in the raddle and wind it carefully on the back roller. Complete dressing the loom as appropriate, setting the ikat sections closer in the reed if wished so that the full resist effect is obtained. The ikat sections may be manipulated before rolling on the warp to stagger the resist areas or produce a diagonal or arrowhead pattern in the weaving. Tie knots in the loops at the back of the warp, or tie tightly across the warp loops (see Fig 37). The fabric can now be woven. Use the dyed weft and a plain weave, or experiment with white and other colours, or with twills for different effects.

Fig 37 *Ties to stagger ikat design*

The colours in this ikat were chosen to show clearly in the illustration, not for their beauty. Direct dyes were used at various strengths to obtain balanced colour values.

Four-colour ikat (Plate 8)

Use Plate 8 and Fig 38 to help follow the description:

1 *Plate 8, top left* Small sample hanks were dyed first to establish and confirm the dye recipes.

2 *Plate 8, top row of warp threads* and *Fig 38, top row of diagram* The ikat sections to be left white were wrapped first, using black tape. These are numbered 1 on the diagram. Next, those to be dyed blue were wrapped, using pink tape to distinguish them. These are numbered 2 on the diagram.

3 *Plate 8, top right* The ikat strips, plain warp sections and the weft yarn, in one hank, were all dyed yellow as the first stage of being coloured green.

4 *Plate 8, second row of threads* and *Fig 38, second row* This shows the situation after the yellow dyeing and removal of the pink wrappings numbered 2. The exposed white areas have become yellow, while the wrapped sections numbered 2 have remained white.

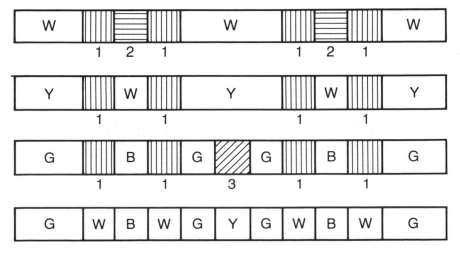

Fig 38 Wrapping and dyeing sequence

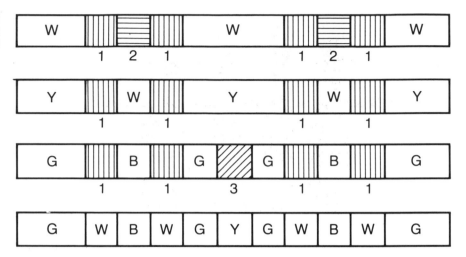

Fig 38 *Wrapping and dyeing sequence*

| W | 1 | 2 | 1 | W | 1 | 2 | 1 | W |

| Y | 1 | W | 1 | Y | 1 | W | 1 | Y |

| G | 1 | B | 1 | G | 3 | G | 1 | B | 1 | G |

| G | W | B | W | G | Y | G | W | B | W | G |

5 *Fig 38, third row* A new wrapping, numbered 3, is added where the ikat is to remain yellow. All the yarn is now dyed in blue, including the ikat strips, plain warp sections, and the weft yarn.

6 *Plate 8, third row* This shows the situation after the blue dyeing. The exposed yellow areas have become green, while the unwrapped white areas (numbered 2) have been coloured blue.

7 *Plate 8, fourth row* and *Fig 38, fourth row* All wrappings are now removed and the final colouring is revealed, with white, yellow, blue and green areas where required on the ikat warp. The weft yarn is green after being over-dyed in blue.

8 *Plate 8, bottom half* This shows the ikat warp threads spread out alongside each other. Some have been pulled and tied to produce chevron and arrowhead patterns, while others have been left as squares. Some of the plain warps have been dyed black.

Weft ikat Weft ikat yarns are produced in a slightly different way – the yarn is hanked around two supports and the required areas then wrapped before dyeing. Fig 39 shows a typical arrangement.

Fig 39 *Weft ikat tying*

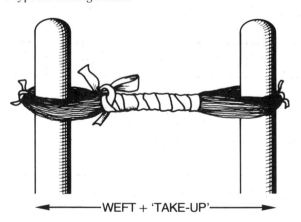

←————WEFT + 'TAKE-UP'————→

As previously mentioned, it is inadvisable to wrap too thick a bundle of yarn as the dye tends to creep beneath the binding. It is usual to dye weft yarn in a series of hanks to avoid this problem.

If the position of the wrapping is altered among the yarns, a number of different ikat patterns will be produced which can then be combined during weaving to build up a more intricate design (see Fig 40). Remember to allow for weft 'take-up' when planning the weft hanks.

Ikat is a fascinating art that presents all sorts of opportunities for innovation in dyeing and yarn manipulation. Many ideas are presented in the books on the subject included in the Bibliography as suggestions for further reading.

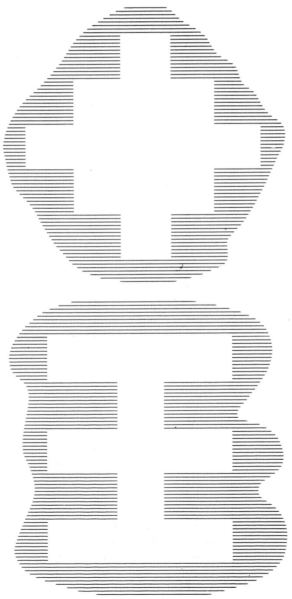

Fig 40 *Different designs for weft ikat*

GLOSSARY

This glossary defines words and expressions used in the text that may not otherwise be explained.

Additive mixing
The progressive combination of optical colours to produce lighter and lighter mixtures, eventually reaching white light.

Affinity
The natural attraction existing between a fibre and a dye, or an attraction created or enhanced by the use of dyebath assistants.

After-image
An optical phenomenon that occurs when the eye is saturated by prolonged viewing of a particular colour and carries that image forward in its complementary colour when the gaze is shifted.

Analagous colours
Those that are in close enough proximity to each other in the spectrum to be in harmony. They appear in the same quadrant of a colour circle.

Bain-marie
An arrangement of dyepots heated simultaneously from one source via a water bath. It often consists of foil 'freezer' containers floating in a tray of water to which heat is applied, and allows a close control of temperature.

Batt
A flat, parallel arrangement of carded fibres as produced by a drum carder.

Bonding
The attachment that occurs between the molecules of a fibre and the molecules of a dye.

Capillaries
The minute internal pores of a fibre into which the dye molecules penetrate.

Carriers
Chemicals used in dyeing some man-made fibres to increase the rate of dye penetration, thus allowing more straightforward dyeing procedures than might otherwise be possible.

Cellulosic
Consisting of, or chemically akin to, cellulose fibres.

Complementary colours
Pairs which when mixed together will produce white light (in the case of optical colours or coloured lights) or near black (in the case of pigment colours). They consist of two primaries together on the one hand, and the remaining

primary on the other, and represent the greatest possible contrast in colour.

Continuous filament	A single fibre produced in an unbroken length. Silk is the only natural example, all others being man-made.
Contrast of tone	An optical phenomenon in which a dark tone appears paler at a boundary with a lighter tone, and vice versa.
Dispersing agent	A substance used mainly with disperse dyes to keep the dye particles evenly distributed in the dye liquor.
Dyebath	The liquor in which fibres and yarns are coloured.
Dyebath assistant	One of a variety of chemicals added to increase dyeing efficiency. They include acids, alkalis and surfactants.
Dyepot/Dyepan	The vessel in which the dyebath is contained.
Exhaustion	The condition in a dyebath in which all dye has been taken up by the fibre, leaving the dye liquor substantially clear.
Fibres	The individual strands of a textile material. In this book they include fleece, yarn and threads.
Hue	The pure colour as found in the spectrum.
Ikat	A system of resist-dyeing threads which are then woven and manipulated to form distinctively patterned fabrics.
Intermediate colour	A colour produced by mixing adjacent primaries and secondaries.
Levelling	Promoting an even take-up of dye throughout a fibre or fabric. Levelling dyes are compounded to feature this characteristic.
Levelling agent	A surfactant added to a dyebath to moderate the rate of dye take-up, thus aiding the production of even or 'level' colouring.
Liquor ratio	The proportion of water to fibre weight in a dyebath.
Mawata Silk	A form in which a cocoon has been opened out and the silk spread as a thin sheet. Many such sheets can be shaped over a dome to produce a mawata 'silk cap'.
Milling	The process of scouring, beating and fulling woollen fabric to achieve a specified amount of shrinkage, and thus its finished dimensions. Milling dyes are designed to maintain a high degree of washfastness under this treatment.
Monochromatic	Of one colour, although there may be variations in tone.
pH	A numerical indication of the acidity or alkalinity of water. The scale runs from 0 to 14, the

mid-point being 7. A pH of 1 is very acid, and a pH of 14 is very alkaline.

Pre-metallised A term applied to a type of acid dye in which a metallic salt is combined with the dye molecule during manufacture. These dyes are also called 'metal complex'.

Primary colour A colour that cannot be made by mixing other colours.

Resist A technique of applying an impervious coating to a fibre or fabric to prevent that part of it receiving dye. A resist is normally applied as dictated by a pattern or design, and removed after dyeing is completed.

Restraining agent A dyebath assistant used to retard the rate of dye transfer to a fibre to promote even colouring.

Rolag A circular arrangement of carded fibres, produced typically by hand carding and used for 'woollen spun' yarns.

Roving A continuous sliver of combed fibre ready for drafting and spinning.

Secondary colour One made by mixing two primaries.

Shade A darkened tone of a colour, obtained by adding black, or by mixing with a complementary colour, or by dyeing on a dark fibre. It is the opposite of a tint. Shades absorb light.

Simultaneous contrast An optical phenomenon in which a colour becomes tinged with the complementary colour of its neighbour.

Staple A short length of fibre, either natural or synthetic, the latter produced by cutting a continuous filament.

Strike The speed at which dye molecules attach to a fibre, especially the initial speed when the two are first brought together in a dyebath.

Stripping agent A chemical that removes dye from a coloured fibre in readiness for redyeing to a different colour; differing stripping agents may be required for different dyes.

Subtractive mixing The progressive combination of pigment colours to produce darker and darker mixtures, eventually reaching a dark grey or brown (but black in theory). It is the opposite of additive mixing.

Successive contrast Occurs when the eye is saturated with a particular colour and then views a different colour. The complementary of the first appears to be superimposed on the second to alter its hue.

Surfactant   A substance used in low concentrations to reduce the surface tension of a dye or other solution. Surfactants are used as wetting and levelling agents, and as detergents.

Suspension   In dyeing terms, an even distribution of undissolved dye particles throughout the volume of a dyebath.

Thickening agent   A substance – typically an alginate – added to a dye solution to thicken it so that it can be sprayed or painted on a fabric or yarn.

Tint   In painting terms, a colour that has been lightened by adding white; in textiles it is a colour that is made paler by being dyed below normal strength on a white fibre or yarn.

Tone   A change in the intensity or gradation of a colour from light to dark, or dark to light.

Value   The intensity of a colour in relation to other colours.

Warp   Threads that are the main structural component of a fabric, and are held under tension on a loom.

Weft   Threads that run across the warp to complete the structure of a fabric, and often help carry the pattern.

Wetting agent   A surfactant used in a wetting bath to reduce the surface tension of the water, enabling it to penetrate the capillary spaces of a fibre in preparation for dyeing.

Working   The deliberate movement of fibres in a dyebath to ensure an even exposure to dye or chemical solutions.

BIBLIOGRAPHY AND FURTHER READING

Books on dyeing

Brown, Pauline, *Embroidery Backgrounds: Painting and Dyeing Techniques* (B. T. Batsford Ltd, 1984) Very useful for the embroiderer; the dyeing techniques could be used on yarns as well as on fabrics.

Davenport, Elsie G., *Your Yarn Dyeing* (Elsie G. Davenport, 1953) Packed with information on the use of natural and synthetic dyes, and colour mixing, but possibly a little dated.

Fox, M. R., *VAT Dyestuffs* (Chapman & Hall, 1946) A comprehensive and technical description of the chemistry of vat dyes.

Giles, Dr C. H., *A Laboratory Course in Dyeing* (Society of Dyers and Colourists, 1974) The basic reference for students of textile dyeing.

Knutson, Linda, *Synthetic Dyes for Natural Fibers* (Madrona Publishers, Seattle, 1982) Useful for further study, especially the chemistry of dyeing, colour mixing, etc.

Ponting, K. G., *A Dictionary of Dyes and Dyeing* (Mills & Boon, 1980) Invaluable reference to natural and synthetic dyeing, It contains a wealth of historical detail and practical information.

Robinson, Stuart and Patricia, *Beginner's Guide to Fabric Dyeing and Printing* (Newnes Technical Books, 1982) Useful information on dyes and chemicals in relation to fabrics, but could be applied to yarns.

Robinson, Stuart, *A History of Dyed Textiles* (Studio Vista, 1969) Good historical information on dyes, fibres and methods of textile dyeing.

Storey, Joyce, *Dyes and Fabrics* (Thames & Hudson, 1978) An excellent book for the serious textile student, with detailed information on dyes and dyeing, and a good chapter on fibres.

Vinroot, Sally, and Chowder, Jennie, *The New Dyer* (Interweave Press Inc, 1985) Covers acid, reactive and disperse dyes, and presents a patented method for colour mixing and analysis.

Books on colour

Albers, Josef, *Interaction of Colour* (University Press Ltd, 1963) A guide and teaching aid for students and artists. Working through the different projects helps one to 'see' and understand colour.

Birren, Faber, *Creative Colour* (Van Nostrand Reinhold, 1961) A basic course on colour harmony. *The Textile Colourist* (Van Nostrand Reinhold, 1980) Very helpful to all textile artists. Teaches the effects of colour mixing in embroidery, weaving, knitting, etc. Many excellent colour plates.

Chevreul, M. E., *The Principles of Harmony and Contrast of Colours* (edited by Faber Birren and published by Van Nostrand Reinhold, 1967, and Garland Publications, 1980) Good historical reading and one of the greatest books written about colour (in 1839). Deals mainly with colour in Gobelin tapestries, hangings and carpets.

Gupthill, Arthur L., *Colour Manual for Artists* (Van Nostrand Reinhold, 1962) Written for artists but equally relevant to textile dyers. Chapters on colour facts, colour mixing and the use of colour charts.

Itten, Johannes, *The Elements of Colour* (Van Nostrand Reinhold, 1971) A simplified and condensed version of Itten's *The Art of Colour*. Invaluable for the serious student.

Klein, Bernat, *Eye for Colour* (Collins, 1965) How to see colour in the environment and use it in textiles.

Munsell, Albert, *A Grammar of Colour* (edited and annotated by Faber Birren and published by Van Nostrand Reinhold, 1969) The treatise of colour harmony.

Society of Dyers and Colourists, *Introducing Colour* (The Society of Dyers and Colourists, 1975) A booklet mainly for teachers, presenting information on light, colour theory and application.

Various authors, *Colour* (Marshall Editions Ltd, 1980) A marvellous book describing the full story of colour – what it is, how we see it, how we use it, how it influences our lives.

General references, including fibres, dyeing and colour

Battenfield, Jackie, *IKAT Techniques* (Van Nostrand Reinhold, 1978) A good introduction to ikat, including design, colour, dyeing, weaving and contemporary work.

Black, Mary E., *The Key to Weaving* (Collier Macmillan Publishers, London, 1945) Mainly weaving, but very useful sections on fibres and colour.

Burkett, M. E., *The Art of the Feltmaker* (M. E. Burkett, 1979) Fascinating history of felt through the ages, with excellent illustrations.

Donald, Kay, *Creative Feltmaking* (Kangaroo Press, 1983) Felt-making described in a simple and interesting way.

Gale, Elizabeth, *From Fibres to Fabrics* (Mills & Boon/Allman & Son, 1968) Detailed information on fibres and their preparation.

Gordon, Beverly, *Feltmaking* (Watson-Gupthill Publications, 1980) Many interesting and unusual ideas.

Hochberg, Bette, *Fibre Facts* (Bette & Bernard Hochberg, 1981) Comprehensive review of natural and synthetic fibres and their physical properties. *Handspinners Handbook* (Bette & Bernard Hochberg, 1976) Descriptions of most natural fibres in relation to spinning.

Howard, Constance, *Embroidery and Colour* (B. T. Batsford, 1976) Excellent practical guidance on the choice and use of colour; helpful to all textile artists.

Jackson, Constance, and Plowman, Judith, *The Woolcraft Book, Spinning, Dyeing and Weaving* (Collins, 1980) Good information on wool and sheep breeds; helpful hints on dye mixing and colour, but with natural dyeing bias.

Justema, William and Doris, *Weaving and Needlecraft Colour Course* (Van Nostrand Reinhold) Experiments with yarn and colour.

Kurtz, Carol S., *Designing for Weaving* (Hastings House, New York, 1981) Contains an excellent chapter on colour theory and application.

Lenor-Larsen, Jack, *The Dyer's Art* (Van Nostrand Reinhold, 1976) A treasure-house of design and colour; many beautiful illustrations of resist dyed yarns and fabric.

Seagroatt, Margaret, *A Basic Textile Book* (Van Nostrand Reinhold, 1975) Excellent information on natural and synthetic fibres and the use of dyes.

Tomita, Jun and Noriko, *Japanese Ikat Weaving* (Routledge & Kegan Paul, 1982) A comprehensive description of the ikat techniques, with a chapter on indigo.

Watson, William, *Textile Design and Colour* (Butterworths, 1920) Excellent for further study into the relationships between colour and fibres in spinning and weaving.

CIBA reviews

1962/5 Hemp
1962/6 Assessment of modification of wool during wet processing
1964/2 Dyeing theory
1964/33 The polyolefins
1965/2 Flax
1965/3 Yarn and thread
1967/2 Artificial silk
1967/4 Japanese resist dyeing techniques
1969/1 Alginates
1969/2 Surfactants
1972/11 Wool
1973/4 Textile printing
1975/1 Cotton

ICI technical information bulletins

1960/545 Chrome after-dyeing
1971/1254 Dyeing wool at high temperature
D. 1573 Procion dyes for cotton yarn dyeing
D. 1600 Procion dyes; exhaust dyeing viscose rayon staple
D. 1616 Procion H-E/H dyes; exhaust dyeing mercerised cotton knitwear
D. 1619 Procion H-E/H dyes; exhaust dyeing unmercerised cotton piece

Magazines and periodicals

Crafts, Crafts Advisory Committee, Waterloo Place, London, SW1Y 4AU, England

Crafts Australia, Crafts Council of Australia, Sydney, NSW 2000, Australia

Fiberarts, Lark Communications, Ashville, NC28801, USA

Handwoven, Interweave Press Inc, Loveland, CO 80537, USA

Journal, Journal of the Society of Dyers and Colourists, Bradford, BD1 2JB, England

Shuttle, Spindle and Dyepot, Handweavers Guild of America Inc, W. Hartford, Conn 06107, USA

Spin-Off, Interweave Press Inc, Loveland, CO 80537, USA

Surface, Surface Design Journal, Oxford, Ohio 45056, USA

The Australian Handweaver and Spinner, Handweavers and Spinners Guild of Australia

The Journal, Quarterly Journal of the Association of Guilds of Spinners, Weavers and Dyers, BCM 963, London WC1N 3XX, England

The Web, New Zealand Spinning, Weaving and Woolcrafts Society, PO Box 255, Balclutha, Otago, NZ

Weavers Journal, Colorado Fiber Centre, Boulder, CO 80306, USA

British Man-made Fibres Federation, 24 Buckingham Gate, London, SW1E 6LB

Information sources

British Wool Marketing Board, Oak Mills, Station Road, Bradford, West Yorkshire, BD14 6JD

Ciba-Geigy Dyestuffs and Chemicals, Rhodes, Middleton, Manchester, M24 4RH

Croda Colours, Brookfoot, Brighouse, West Yorkshire, HD6 2QZ

Durham Chemicals Distributors Ltd, 55–7 Glengall Road, London, SE15 6NQ

Dylon International Ltd, Worsley Bridge Road, Lower Sydenham, London, SE26 5HD

ICI plc, Organics Division, PO Box 42, Hexagon House, Blackley, Manchester, M9 3DA

Sandoz Chemicals, Calverley Lane, Horsforth, Leeds, LS18 4RP

Shirley Developments Ltd, PO Box 6, 856 Wilmslow Road, Manchester, M20 8SA

Society of Dyers and Colourists, PO Box 244, Perkin House, 82 Gratton Road, Bradford, BD1 2JB

SUPPLIERS

Ashill Craft Studio (Gill Dalby), Dulverton, Somerset, TA22 9RT. Dyeing utensils and equipment; Methuen Handbook of Colour.

Colour Craft (Elizabeth Lewis), Brownings Farm, Blackboys, Uckfield, East Sussex. Kemtex dyes and dyekits; utensils and equipment.

Durham Chemicals Distributors Ltd, 55–7 Glengall Road, London, SE15 6NQ. Synthetic dyes of all types; dyeing chemicals.

Dylon International Ltd, Worsley Bridge Road, Lower Sydenham, London, SE26 5HD. 'Household' and craft dyes.

Fibrecrafts (Anna Bowers), Style Cottage, Lower Eashing, Godalming, Surrey, GU7 2QD. Acid levelling dyes; dyekits; scales and other equipment.

Kemtex Services Ltd, Victoria Works, Wilton Street, Denton, Manchester, M34 3ND. Acid and reactive dyes.

Spectrum Dyes (Roy Russell), Three Ply House, 57a Lant Street, London, SE1 1QN. The Russell Dye System; Spectrum acid and reactive dyes.

Wood and Wool (Frances and Tony Tompson), 2 High Meads, Wheathampstead, Herts, AL4 8DN. Acid milling and metal-complex, reactive, direct and disperse, dyes; dyekits; dyeing equipment.

Dryad Ltd, PO Box 38, Northgates, Leicester, LE1 9BU. Various fibres and yarns.

Fibrecrafts (Anna Bowers), Style Cottage, Lower Eashing, Godalming, Surrey, GU7 2QD. Various fibres.

Graupner, A. K., Corner House, Valley Road, Bradford 1, Yorks. Wool, mohair and other yarns.

Haldane & Co (Woodturners) Ltd, Gateside, Cupar, Fife, KY14 7ST. Various fibres.

Hall, William and Co (Monsall) Ltd, 177 Stanley Road, Cheadle Hulme, Cheadle, Cheshire, SK8 6RF. Cotton, linen and wool yarns.

Handweavers Studio and Gallery Ltd, 29 Haroldstone Road, London, E17 7AN. Various fibres and yarns.

Hermit Wools Ltd, 89 Caledonia Street, Bradford, West Yorkshire. Knitting wools.

Hunter of Brora, TM Hunter Ltd, Brora, Sutherland, KW9 6NA, Scotland. Scottish tweed yarns for weaving; white rovings.

Hyslop, Bathgate & Co, Victoria Works, Galashiels, Scotland. Wool, silk and mohair yarns for weaving and knitting.

Nottingham Educational Supplies, 17 Ludlow Hill Road, West Bridgford, Nottingham, NG2 6HD. Various yarns for embroidery, weaving and dyeing.

Rowan Yarns, Green Lane Mill, Washpit, West Yorkshire, HD7 1RW. Various yarns including chenille, mainly for knitting.

Silk for Handspinners (Sue Harris), The Mill, Tregoyd Mill, Three Cocks, Brecon, Powys, LD3 0SW. Silk fibres, cocoons, Mawata silk, etc.

Tasseltips, Wood Farm, Ubbeston, Suffolk, IP19 0EU. Angora rabbit wool.

Texere Yarns, College Mill, Barkerend Road, Bradford, West Yorkshire. Yarns for knitting and weaving; some fibres; silk.

Wingham Wool Work, Carlton House, 70 Main Street, Wentworth, Rotherham, South Yorkshire, S62 7TN. Many different fibres and some yarns.

Yarncraft (Angela Lodge), Three Ply House, 57a Lant Street, London, SE1 1QN. All types of undyed yarn for weaving, knitting and crochet.

Cerulean Blue Ltd, PO Box 21168, Seattle, WA98111. Also equipment. **United**

Earth Guild Dept, One Tingle Alley, Asheville, NC 28001. **States of**

Fab Dec, 3553 Old Post Road, San Angelo, TX 76904. **America**

Flynn's, Box 11304, San Francisco, CA 94101. *Synthetic*

Keystone-Ingham Corpn, PO Box 669, Artesia, CA 90701. (Large quantities *dyes* only.)

Pro Chemical and Dye Inc, PO Box 14, Somerset, MA 02716.

Straw into Gold Inc, 3006 San Pablo Ave, Berkeley, CA 94702. Also equipment.

Textile Resources, PO Box 34786, Los Angeles, CA 90034.

Yarn Barn, 918 Massachusetts St, Lawrence, Kansas, 66044.

Clothworks, 132 Powell Street, Vancouver, BC, V6A 1G1. **Canada**

Espo Dyes Inc, RR2, Tottenham, Ontario, LOG 1WO. *Synthetic dyes*

Fiber Hut, Site 2, Box 37, RR8, Calgary, Alberta, T2J 2T9.

Helen Koop, 662 Warren Road, London, Ontario, N6H 2V5.

Parkson Distributing, PO Box 374, Clarkson, PO Mississauga, Ontario, L5J 3Y2.

Sun Bench Fibres, c/o Hanlo Lubben, 49612 Larsen Road, Sardis, British Columbia, V2R 1B1.

Telio and Co, 5800 Rue St Denis, Suite 502, Montreal, Quebec, H2S 3L5.

Wool 'n' Wheel, RR1, Ilderton, Ontario, NOM 2AO.

Wool Palette, 256 Naismith Drive, Box 1135, Almonte, Ontario, KOA 1AO.

Albright & Wilson, 610 St Kilda Road, Melbourne, Vic. 3001. Levelling **Australia** agents, Calgon, softeners, detergents. **and**

Ajax Chemicals, Short Street, Auburn, NSW 2144. Hamlet Street, Chelten **New Zealand** ham, Vic. 3192. Chemicals for mordants and dyeing operations. *Synthetic dyes*

Bayer Australia, 47–67 Wilson Street, Botany, NSW 2019. 633–647 Springvale Road, Glen Waverley, Vic. 3150. Dyes, levelling agents, auxiliary agents etc.

Robert Bryce, 145–147 Glenlyon Road, Brunswick, Vic. 3056. Chemicals, dyestuffs, auxiliary agents.

Ciba-Geigy Australia Ltd, 235 Settlement Road, Thomastown, Vic. 3074. 14 Orion Road, Lane Cove, NSW 2066. Dyes, auxiliary agents, detergents.

Croda Chemicals, 28 Flockhart Street, Abbotsford, Vic. 3067. Chemicals, dyestuffs, auxiliary agents, detergents.

Dye Services, 25 Duke Street, Abbotsford, Vic. 3067. Dyes, chemicals, auxiliary agents, detergents.

Hodgsons Dye Agencies Pty Ltd, 24 William Street, Balaclava, Vic. 3183. Dyes, auxiliary agents, detergents.

Hoechst Australia Ltd, 606 St Kilda Road, Melbourne, Vic. 3001. Dyes, auxiliary agents, detergents.

Sandoz Australia Pty Ltd, 675 Warrigal Road, Chadstone, Vic. 3148. Dyes, chemicals, auxiliary agents, detergents.

H. B. Selby, 352 Ferntree Gully Road, Mt. Waverley, Vic. 3149. Chemicals for mordants, glassware, thermometers.

G. J. Vago & Sons Pty Ltd, 58 Epsom Road, Rosebery, NSW 2018. Dyes, auxiliaries, detergents.

A. E. Walker, Beverage Drive, Tullamarine, Vic. 3043. Chemicals for dyeing and mordants.

Yorkshire Chemicals, Rooney Street, Burnley, Vic. 3121. Dyes, auxiliary agents, detergents etc.

Jalfon Chemicals Ltd, PO Box 26, Oneroa, Waiheke Island, NZ.

APPENDIX

Conversion tables

Grams Millilitres	to to	Ounces Fluid Ounces
28.4	1	0.04
56.7	2	0.07
85.0	3	0.11
113.4	4	0.14
142.0	5	0.18
284.0	10	0.35
568.0	20	0.70
852.0	30	1.06
1,136.0	40	1.41
1,420.0	50	1.76
2,849.0	100	3.52
5,680.0	200	7.04
8,520.0	300	10.56
11,360.0	400	14.08
14,200.0	500	17.61

Millilitres per Litre		Fluid Ounces per Gallon
6.24	1	0.16
12.48	2	0.32
18.72	3	0.48
24.96	4	0.64
31.20	5	0.80
62.40	10	1.60
124.80	20	3.20
187.20	30	4.80
249.60	40	6.40
312.00	50	8.00

Centimetres		Inches
2.54	1	0.39
5.08	2	0.79
7.62	3	1.18
10.16	4	1.57
12.70	5	1.97
25.40	10	3.94
50.80	20	7.87
76.20	30	11.81
101.60	40	15.75

Litres		Pints
0.57	1	1.76
1.14	2	3.52
1.70	3	5.28
2.27	4	7.04
2.84	5	8.80
5.69	10	17.60
11.36	20	35.20
17.05	30	52.79
22.73	40	70.39
28.41	50	87.99

ACKNOWLEDGEMENTS

The authors would like to acknowledge their indebtedness to all the friends who helped in this book, and especially the undermentioned.

Roy Russell, who first introduced us to the delights of synthetic dyeing, and inspired us to explore its mysteries and possibilities. Arthur Creighton, for his patience and skill in photography. Rasma Budins and Hilary Goddard, textile designers and lecturers, for their encouragement and advice regarding the colour sections.

For reading the manuscript and practical advice on the dyeing and safety techniques:

Alan Blue and Laura Thompson, of Sandoz Chemicals. John Howlett, of Durham Chemicals. Paul Thompson, of Dylon International. Greg Bungay and P. F. Meal, HM Factory Inspectors.

For generously supplying dye samples, publications and technical information:

Messrs CIBA-Geigy, Croda Colours, Durham Chemicals, Dylon International, ICI Organics, Sandoz Chemicals.

We would also like to remember Anna Polanski, whose enthusiasm for colour and design has been an inspiration and a beacon.

INDEX